INTIMACY DI|
FOR THEATRE

Intimacy Directing for Theatre provides much-needed strategies on how teachers and artists can do intimacy work in the classroom and rehearsal room that is safe and just.

This book puts forth intimacy work that is based on human rights and consent for everyone, fully integrating justice with intimacy directing. It offers practical advice on how instructors can do intimacy work in their courses and productions that is based on consent, and racial and gender justice. Each chapter is written by an instructor and professional practitioner who offers their perspective and experience on how to cultivate a space that is safe and intersectional, as well as respectful of students' race, gender, sexual orientation, and other integral modes of identity. Chapters contain "low stakes" exercises that help to keep the rehearsal room safe, consensual, and inclusive.

Intimacy Directing for Theatre is an excellent resource for Theatre & Performance instructors and practitioners who want to create and sustain a culture of consent in their classrooms and rehearsal rooms.

Dr. Ayshia Mackie-Stephenson is an intimacy director, actor, scholar, and award-winning write from Brooklyn, NY. With an MFA from CalArts and a PhD from UMass Amherst, she uses performance to investigate sexuality, race, and human rights. Her critical and creative work appears in Black Camera, Qualitative Inquiry, Boston University Press, International Review of Qualitative Research, Theatre Topics, Howlround and Research in Drama Education. Dr. Ayshia has directed or intimacy directed productions at The Huntington, Fresh Ink Theatre, Jewel Box Theatre in NYC, Arts at the Armory (Somerville), The Rockwell, and the DC Black Theatre & Arts Festival. She is Assistant Professor of Art and Performance Studies at Xavier University of Louisiana, hosts Dr. AyshiaTV (a YouTube channel on radical performance), and is the Founder of AfroGoddess Theatre.

INTIMACY DIRECTING FOR THEATRE

Creating a Culture of Consent in the Classroom and Beyond

Edited by Dr. Ayshia Mackie-Stephenson

Routledge
Taylor & Francis Group

NEW YORK AND LONDON

Designed cover image: Nikkole Salter and Postell Pringle in The Huntington's production of *Our Daughters, Like Pillars* by Kirsten Greenidge. Directed by Kimberly Senior. Photo by T Charles Erickson.

First published 2024
by Routledge
605 Third Avenue, New York, NY 10158

and by Routledge
4 Park Square, Milton Park, Abingdon, Oxon, OX14 4RN

Routledge is an imprint of the Taylor & Francis Group, an informa business

Library of Congress Cataloging-in-Publication Data
Names: Mackie-Stephenson, Ayshia, editor.
Title: Intimacy directing for theatre : creating a culture of consent in the
    classroom and beyond / edited by Ayshia Mackie-Stephenson.
Description: New York, NY : Routledge, 2024. | Includes
    bibliographical references.
Identifiers: LCCN 2023008371 (print) | LCCN 2023008372 (ebook) |
    ISBN 9781032333793 (hardback) | ISBN 9781032333762 (paperback) |
    ISBN 9781003319399 (ebook)
Subjects: LCSH: Sex in the theater. | Intimacy (Psychology) in the theater. |
    Theater rehearsals. | Theater—Production and direction—Social aspects.
Classification: LCC PN2071.S49 I58 2024 (print) | LCC PN2071.S49 (ebook) |
    DDC 792.02/33—dc23/eng/20230522
LC record available at https://lccn.loc.gov/2023008371
LC ebook record available at https://lccn.loc.gov/2023008372

ISBN: 978-1-032-33379-3 (hbk)
ISBN: 978-1-032-33376-2 (pbk)
ISBN: 978-1-003-31939-9 (ebk)

DOI: 10.4324/9781003319399

Typeset in Joanna
by Apex CoVantage, LLC

For survivors of sexual violence, I hear you, I see you, I love you.

CONTENTS

ACKNOWLEDGEMENTS

I have to start by thanking my wonderful and supportive husband, Carlin. Thank you for all the advice, feedback, tea, and foot rubs when this felt so hard to do. I love you always.

I also want to thank my mother, Beverly Stephenson, for your love and loyalty; my best friend and theatre partner Brian Moore-Ward for supporting my work and creating human rights theatre with me in Boston; Estelle Disch for your kindness and for teaching me how to write; Leda Cooks for having my back and believing in me, the amazing women of Intimacy Directors & Coordinators, Tonia Sina, Alicia Rodis, and Claire Warden (thank you for your mentorship), who offered me a scholarship for the week long intimacy intensive that changed my life; the contributors to this book who deliver such heartwarming brilliance with their words and work; Antonio Ocampo-Guzman of Northeastern University; The Huntington Theatre for offering me work that informed these chapters; Stacey Walker, Routledge Publisher, for your excitement about this project; and my lovely editor Lucia Accorsi (Senior Editorial Assistant), thank you for your kindness and patience.

1

INTRODUCTION

Dr. Ayshia Mackie-Stephenson

This book is for teachers – teachers who create art and artists who teach and lead. We need tools to navigate the revolution of intimacy direction that has surged the field of theatre and other modes of performance. Anyone leading a space in which theatrical intimacy and consent practices exist, can use this book as a guide. In this introductory chapter, I will speak to what intimacy direction is, why/when to hire a professional, why consent matters, and the importance of consent workshops. Sample consent workshop activities are also provided. This book offers much needed strategies on how teachers can do intimacy work in the classroom and rehearsal room that is safe *and* just. The institution of academia has such an effect on the performance field (BFAs, MFAs, etc.) and for many young artists/actors, it is a formative experience. All too often artists and academics are pitted against each other or do not see ourselves as allies for one reason or another. Yet many teachers are artists, and artists who lead are also teachers; my hope is that both can see themselves

DOI: 10.4324/9781003319399-1

in this book. I can say that I've learned a lot from working arm-to-arm with many amazing artist activists who are inside and outside of academia. I'm hoping that our thoughts here will ignite a conversation and more unity between two entangled spheres of the theatre world. When artists and teachers work together, we affect and transform spaces for ourselves and the world.

Bodily integrity is a human right and actors are human beings. This book puts forth intimacy work that is based in human rights and consent for everyone. It offers strategies on how teachers can do intimacy work in the classroom and rehearsal room that is based in consent and racial and gender justice. Just to be clear, intimacy direction is not in the business of pornography, however, doing any theatrical intimacy work with minors is a different situation because of child pornography laws. This book does not address doing intimacy work with minors, if you teach minors then please do your due diligence to protect children. The book is for theatre teachers in academia (higher education) and professional spaces. Most chapters are written by teachers who are also professional artists and will offer their take on how to cultivate a space that is safe and intersectional, respecting students' race, gender, sexual orientation and other integral modes of identity. Contributors will also offer "low stakes" exercises that help them to keep the rehearsal room safe, consensual and inclusive. As the editor, I want to be clear that I, along with several contributors, am trained by Intimacy Directors and Coordinators (here-in-after IDC), while other contributors are associated with and trained by other theatrical intimacy organizations. We are all in this together, as we are all out there doing the work in our classrooms and rehearsal rooms to make humans safer.

This book acknowledges and honors intimacy direction's foundation in Black feminism, third world feminism and Black critical theory – the basis for intersectional justice in the U.S. and beyond. The acknowledgment of this truth is already an act of justice. Let me begin with what intimacy directing is and connect that to where it comes from; it's a relatively new field in theatre and film that has taken the industry by storm. Intimacy in storytelling can include incidents of simulated sex, kissing, performance nudity, death or mourning, and other sexual, physical, and emotionally intensive acts of a private and/or sensitive nature. This book advocates for all intimacy work to be intersectional. Intimacy direction was birthed by The Me Too Movement – a landmark 21st Century movement created by a Black woman. Therefore, the history of intimacy directing certainly calls upon a human rights legacy and a legacy to end White supremacy. Intimacy work in theatre, film, and other performance is inspired by the Me Too Movement, which was created by Black American activist Tarana Burke to end sexual violence against women.[1] Burke realized how gender, race, culture, privilege, and socio-economics impact how a woman is put at risk for sexual violence and a woman's ability to speak up regarding her trauma with said violence. This is intersectionality. It's no coincidence that some of the best ID trainings have connected intimacy work with other callings for justice. For example, according to Colleen Hughes, "Kimberlé Crenshaw has informed much of IDC's curriculum."[2] Kimberlé Crenshaw, a Black professor and attorney whose work is based in U.S. law, third world feminism, and Black critical theory, coined the term "intersectionality" over 30 years ago in 1989.[3] Intersectionality is an analytical framework for understanding how aspects of a person's social and political identities combine to create different modes of discrimination and privilege. There is no intimacy directing without intersectionality. We need it to bring justice to the work and the people.

The fundamentals of intimacy direction were created by Tonia Sina, Intimacy Director at Intimacy Directors and Coordinators (IDC) and former Co-Founder of Intimacy Directors International (IDI); Alicia Rodis, Intimacy Director/Coordinator at IDC and Co-Founder of IDI; and Siobhan Richardson, also a Co-Founder of IDI. IDC is an institution that pioneers the best practices for simulated intimacy; there are many in the field now also doing excellent and ethical work, such as Intimacy Coordinators of Color and Theatrical Intimacy Education (TIE). Kaja Dunn, Associate Professor of Anti-Racist and Culturally Competent Practice at Carnegie Mellon University's School of Drama and Associate Faculty at Theatrical Intimacy Education, is the pioneer of cultural competency training for intimacy directing work.[4] When she was at UNC Charlotte, professor Kaja Dunn earned a Kennedy Center honor for her work addressing equity in theater education. Her work in race and choreography training has been critical to the way that intimacy directing is used to respect all bodies.

Intimacy directing is a **human rights movement**. When I assisted Claire Warden, Intimacy Coordinator/Director and Creative Officer at IDC and my mentor, in a 2019 Stagesource Intimacy Intensive, she said something I'll never forget. Claire said, "actors are human beings." It literally blew my mind. So obvious yet not so obvious. How often and how intentionally is that knowledge routinely put to practice? This book claims the understanding of human rights as essential to doing intimacy work. Human rights are

> rights inherent to all human beings, regardless of race, sex, nationality, ethnicity, language, religion, or any other status. Human rights include the right to life and liberty, freedom from slavery and torture, freedom of opinion and expression, the right to work and education, and many more. Everyone is entitled to these rights, without discrimination.[5]

Intimacy directors are advocates. Intimacy directors work in live performance (i.e. theatre), while intimacy coordinators work in film. Both advocate for actors – both are leaders in helping directors and actors to tell stories authentically and safely. Intimacy directors and intimacy coordinators are also thought of as **intimacy choreographers**. According to Intimacy Coordinators of Color, intimacy choreographers are "responsible for the consensual crafting and staging of stories of sex, race, disability, religion, or age with appropriate cultural context and competency. They consult on scenes with loaded, heightened, or charged content that draws on the actor's identity."[6] An intimacy director assumes the responsibility of holding the room and caring for the safety of the actors and everyone else in it. For these reasons, I recommend using this book to understand what intimacy directing is: to begin to build a culture of consent in your classrooms and rehearsal rooms, for low-stakes scene work in the classroom if you already have some training, as a supplement to a certified intimacy director working on the play your team is staging, as a supplement to a certified intimacy coordinator for the film you are creating (the medium is different but many of the principles still apply), as a means for you to strengthen your own training and to learn from other intimacy directors in the field. Training for intimacy direction includes many facets – I would begin by taking courses at an established institute such as TIE or IDC. Beyond coursework in intimacy directing, training should also include racial and gender justice education, movement and directing pedagogy, acting theory, consent and sexual harassment education, Title IX, mental health first aid training/certification, first aid certification, several class hours learning about intimacy direction, structured shadowing and mentorship, and experience in the field – either leading consent workshops and/or being hired as an ID for increasingly heightened pieces. Certification as an ID is also a pathway for training and includes much of that and often more.

This book is no way a replacement for an intimacy director. Nothing can replace a highly trained intimacy director in your classroom and rehearsal room. I'm so happy that so many theatre and film artists are taking intimacy workshops and classes: basic training serves us all. However, if you are not highly trained within a specific form of intimacy work, then hire someone who is (and if you can, shadow them to learn more). I started training with intimacy work because I was writing and directing plays on race and sexuality, such as *Brooklyn Bedroom* and *Venus Hottentot: A Short Play* (see Figure 1.1 to see the Black woman playing Sara Baartman and the White man representing Alexander Dunlop who brought her to Europe). I was writing and directing scenes where actors were hugging, kissing, touching, and simulating sex, yet I did know how to choreograph these scenes in safe and authentic ways, so I decided to stop and seek help and get training. I wanted to help keep my actors safe. I also wanted to make my simulated scenes look hot (if the intimacy was consensual) and authentic and honest. I wanted to know how to approach interracial romance stories. How do you guide two people with marked bodies through intimacy?

Before I was certified in intimacy direction, I made mistakes, I put actors in risky situations, and so have you. I still do make mistakes; we are all learning and remembering that we don't know it all actually helps to keep the people we are trying to protect safe. The mistakes before my training were more dangerous because I didn't even know that I didn't know. However, I went from not knowing any better to working for The Huntington Theatre and being told repeatedly that I'm needed in the

Figure 1.1 Talya Sogoba (left) and Callum LaFrance (right) in Venus Hottentot: A
    Short Play

Photo credit by Brian Moore-Ward.

room. This is only possible with intense training, experience doing the
work, confidence, and a real sense of humbleness to serve others.

Without a highly trained intimacy director, the potential for harm is
too great. As my colleague and co-author, Charlie Baker, states:

> I cannot emphasize this enough: While certification is not necessary
> for working in intimacy direction, TRAINING WITHIN THE FIELD IS.
> I continue to hear, from actors, about intimacy directors working in
> Chicago without training, and the kind of ineffective (and harmful)
> practices and absences from rehearsals it leads to. I'm disappointed
> in those positioning themselves as intimacy directors, and on theat-
> ers for not doing their research in who they hire. Fight direction cou-
> pled with sensitivity training isn't intimacy direction. Best intentions
> are not training. Directors also need to be better set up for success in
> working with intimacy directors, but that's a separate story.[7]

The next chapter speaks to the latter conundrum: directors do need to know that intimacy directors/choreographers are nothing to fear, we are here to support and collaborate in the theatre making process.

Bring in an intimacy director to do a consent workshop for your class, to help ground your classroom in basic consent language. Also, hire an intimacy director to be at the very first rehearsal of a show because this allows them to set a climate of consent in the room. Building a culture of consent keeps the team safe and helps them to be more productive because they have the tools to communicate and advocate for themselves and one another. Consent matters because actors are human beings and intimacy direction is a human rights movement. There is no one way to tell a story. There's always a way to tell a story that speaks to what the playwright/director wants *and* respects the boundaries of the actor. Consent and consensual culture need to be taught and not assumed. This is why it is imperative that the cast *and* crew are present for the training. When everyone is trained in consent language, it forms a consent culture and a safer room. Consent workshops also help our actors to have the vocabulary to advocate for themselves, set boundaries, and say "No" as readily as "Yes."

The Pillars,[8] as put forth by IDC, have been critical to my journey with intimacy directing work. There are five of them and they are defined here:

- Context: "Before any choreography can be considered, there must be first an understanding of the story and the given circumstances surrounding a scene of intimacy." Story is really everything. What is the story and what kind of choreography will serve it?

- Consent: "Before any scene of intimacy can be addressed, consent must be established between the actors." Consent can only come from the person receiving the action and is not a stationary concept, meaning that it can be given or taken away at any point. What boundaries does the actor need to move forward in this moment, in future moments?

- Communication: "There must be open and continuous communication between the director, intimacy director, stage management and actors." Communication is essential to all of the steps and is verbal and nonverbal in nature. What needs to be said/illustrated to help the actor tell this story?

- Choreography: "Each scene of intimacy must be choreographed, and that choreography will be adhered to for the entire production." Choreography is intimacy direction, crafting movement is what ID's do. What choreography will speak to the specificity of the story and keep the actors safe?

- Closure: "At the end of every rehearsal or scene of intimacy, actors are encouraged to develop a closing moment between them to signify the ending of the work." Closure is critical to the mental health of actors. What quick activity/gesture can the actors do to connect and leave the work in the room? (See Endnote 8 for more information regarding The Pillars.)

Tips & Activities

Important Note: you might find that a few of the same exercises are shared by the book authors. We decided that this is good pedagogy practice to see different variations of an activity, it provides you with more options and shows how teachers can and should adjust activities to work for us and our students.

Classroom Consent Tips

1. Set the vocabulary for the room: bring in an intimacy director to do a consent workshop for students in your class or production – help ground cast and crew in basic consent language.

2. Discuss The Pillars: what do they mean for the students? How do they pair with the students' experiences with life, theatre, and beyond? How do The Pillars relate to the play, the scene work? What are The Pillars relationship to some of the course concepts (i.e. social justice, monologue, cultural ideas on race, gender, sexuality, etc.)? How do they relate to Viewpoints (or other acting method)?

3. Set an exit strategy/self-care: for a virtual class, students can turn off their camera. For in person, give them the option to step out of the circle, partner work, and/or rehearsal etc., and if they need to, out of the room. If there is a T.A., have them check on the student if the

student stepped out. If there is no T.A., designate/rotate a student(s) to help you hold the room. Actors must know that they can withdraw their consent at any time.

Consent Exercises

1. Try the Consent Circle:[9] this is a low stakes way to help your actors feel empowered, set their boundaries and learn to say "no" without guilt or shame.[10]

   a. Everyone involved stands in a circle together.

   b. To model, the teacher (X) can put their right arm and hand out and call someone's name in the circle (Y).

   c. Y can say No or Yes.

   d. If Y says No, then X extends their arm/hand again and calls another name until someone says Yes.

   e. If Y says Yes, then X (the teacher in this case) can walk over to them and stand to the side of them. Now it's Y's turn to extend their arm/hand and call someone. (When Y is able to move, X takes Y's place in the circle.)

   f. This continues until everyone in the circle has been called at least once. This game is most beneficial when done a few times.

   g. Virtual: the "circle" is the gallery view on Zoom or other platform, everyone can raise their hands and take them down until everyone has gone. Instead of standing next to the person, X gets to look at Y for a count of five (silent counting), then will give a thumbs up.

   h. Reflect (at the end or after the first/second round): which pillars are at work (Consent, Communication, etc.)?

How does it feel to say "no"? Why/how is there a negative context associated with the world "no?" How can "no" become a more neutral response? How can "no" build trust, solidarity, intimacy?

2. Walk around:[11]

   a. This works with a bigger class, 10 or more students. Have students walk around in the space. As they pass someone else, they must decide 1) will I make eye contact with the person OR keep walking, and 2) if I decide to make eye contact, then will I decide to stop and shake their hand OR keep walking?

b. Reflect afterwards and discuss what happened and how it felt to consistently negotiate consent and use only nonverbal communication.

More work with The Pillars:

3. Put students into partners and ask them to use communication to choreograph a 30 second scene that illustrates consent.

4. Tell the partners/group to choose Communication, Consent, Choreography, Context, or Closure. Let the partners/group come up with a 1 minute scene that illustrates the pillar.

5. Give them a context or have them come up with a list of them for the class to use (i.e. coming home from work and greeting family, mother celebrating with daughter at her baby shower). Have them use communication, consent, and choreography to illustrate the context.

6. Always do metacognitive work with students. Reflect with students: what sorts of things came up for them in doing these activities? How can this work inform their work as actors/performers? What additional exercises might be helpful for their consent journey?

Notes

1 "Tarana Burke Founder." *Me Too.* https://metoomvmt.org/get-to-know-us/tarana-burke-founder/.

2 Colleen Hughes, IDC certified ID, choreographer, and teaching artist. See Chapter 8 of this book.

3 Jessica Steinrock, "Intimacy Direction: A New Role in Contemporary Theater Making." 25–27.

4 Kaja Dunn, to learn more about her groundbreaking work go to Chapter 6 in this book.

5 "Global Issues: Human Rights." *United Nations*, n.d. www.un.org/en/global-issues/human-rights.

6 Intimacy Coordinators of Color. www.intimacycoordinatorsofcolor.com.

7 To learn more about Charlie Baker's thoughts and work, see Chapter 7.

8 IDI, *The Pillars*. https://docs.wixstatic.com/ugd/924101_2e8c624bcf3941 66bc0443c1f35efe1d.pdf.

9 This activity is from the Intimacy Choreographer's Intensive at The Eugene O'Neill February 2019.

10 Ms. Percy shares her version of the Consent Circle in Ch 10.

11 This is based upon an activity learned from the Intimacy Choreographer's Intensive at The Eugene O'Neill February 2019.

2

FROM DIRECTOR TO DIRECTOR

WHY INTIMACY DIRECTION IS A NECESSITY

Kimberly Senior

Dear Fellow Director

Yes, you! Theatre maker, storyteller, healer of hearts, agitator of the spirits! You who are on your journey – whether just beginning or continuing to discover decades later. You who have dedicated your life to uncovering the intricacies of humanity, to the endless study of why we do the things we do. You who traffics in intimacy – craving it, denying it, seeking it, reveling in it. I'm writing to you today because if I don't, I will have failed you. I will have kept the most important secret about making theatre today from the very people who will benefit from it the most.

You need an Intimacy Director.

We understand the word "intimacy" when we're speaking of sexual or physical relations. We think about intimacy when we talk about closeness. We know that to be intimate with something is to know it well. Intimacy can also include our experience of grief. Intimacy includes all sexual, physical, and emotional acts that are of a private

DOI: 10.4324/9781003319399-2

or sensitive nature. In storytelling, this can include incidents of death or mourning, simulated sex, kissing, performance nudity, and other sexual, physical, and emotionally intensive acts of a private and/or sensitive nature. As storytellers on both the stage and in the classroom, we will be navigating how to create simulations of these experiences in a way that keeps all of our collaborators safe. We are working with actors and students who are holding the humanity of their character in their hearts and minds while protecting their own humanity. Enter the Intimacy Director.

Since our subject matter navigates the human experience, we're often telling stories with kissing, with intercourse, with (in my latest play) fellatio in an automobile. If it happens in life, it's bound to happen on stage at some point. If you've imagined it happening in life (as with previously stated fellatio), it's bound to happen on stage.

And these are just examples of a sexual nature. What about the moment a superior accidentally brushes by their employee? Or estranged siblings are reunited? Or a father tries to find his way to express his love to his son in a society that favors toxic masculinity? If you've witnessed it happening in life, it's bound to happen on stage at some point.

And these are just examples of a physical nature. What about the quiet between sisters? What about a marriage of fifty years passing each other in the kitchen each morning? What about the experience of grief in a public space? What about high school friends who find love later in life? If you've dreamed of it happening in life, yeah, people are going to write plays about it.

You're nodding along to my letter, so excited to get a piece of mail (book) you can hold in your hand. But . . . wait a minute. Isn't that the Director's job? To craft all these intimacies? The short answer is yes. The long answer is no. Rewind. We should probably start at the beginning. What does a director actually do?

According to Wikipedia:

A **theatre director** or **stage director** is a professional in the theatre field who oversees and orchestrates the mounting of a theatre production such as a play, opera, dance, drama, musical theatre performance, etc. by unifying various endeavors and aspects of production. The director's function is to ensure the quality and completeness of theatre production and to lead the members of the creative team into realizing their artistic vision for it. The director thereby collaborates with a team of creative individuals and other staff to coordinate research and work on all the aspects of the production.[1]

I find this definition a bit incomplete (thanks Wikipedia!). I love that we collaborate and unify. I love that we ensure quality and completeness. However, we're also stewards of the play. We safeguard the story. We nourish its journey from the page to the stage with our team of artists (see Figure 2.1 for an example of Kimberly Senior working with actors to nourish and safeguard the story).

Figure 2.1 In rehearsal for *How to Make an American Son* by Christopher Oscar Peña at Arizona Theatre Company

Photo credit: Sean Daniels.

We are leaders who model behavior for all who encounter us. I think of one of my favorite Buddhist stories:

> "I was once invited to teach with Sakyong Mipham Rinpoche, my teacher's eldest son, in a situation where it wasn't exactly clear what my status was. Sometimes I was treated as a big deal who should come in through a special door and sit in a special seat. Then I'd think, *Okay, I'm a big deal.* I'd start running with that idea and come up with big-deal notions about how things should be. Then I'd get the message, *Oh, no, no, no. You should just sit on the floor and mix with everybody and be one of the crowd.* Okay. So now the message was that I should just be ordinary, not set myself up or be the teacher. But as soon as I was getting comfortable with being humble, I would be asked to do something special that only big deals did. This was a painful experience because I was always being insulted and humiliated by my own expectations. As soon as I was sure of how it should be, so I could feel secure, I would get a message that it should be the other way. Finally I said to the Sakyong, *This is really hurting. I just don't know who I'm supposed to be*, and he said, *Well, you have to learn to be big and small at the same time.*"[2]

When I think about this in terms of Directing, I think when I am being "big" I am acting on behalf of something. I am speaking on behalf of the play, or the institution, or the idea. When I am being "small" it's just, well, me . . . in conversation with an actor on scene work, or an Intimacy Director on the storytelling of the scene.

Being Big and Small is a brilliant tenet of leadership. However, I think the most important part of being a Director is that we are advocates for the artists. As Director, we are the immune system of this gorgeous body called "the play." And all of our artists are the amazing organs held within. Let's consider what the actors are called to do.

> "Grief and rage- you need to contain that, to put a frame around it, where it can play itself out without you or your kin having to die. There is a theory that watching unbearable stories about other people lost in grief and rage is good for you- may cleanse you of your darkness. Do you want to go down to the pits of yourself all alone? Not much. What if an actor could do it for you? Isn't that

why they are called actors? They act for you. You sacrifice them to action." – Anne Carson[3]

They're diving into their grief, their rage, their joy, their sorrow, their lust, their vulnerability – in public! Right in front of us. Sacrificing themselves. I believe it is our job, the Director's job, to give the actors everything possible to make sure they feel emotionally and physically safe while sacrificing themselves to give us stories of our own lives. It is our job to make sure their work in every stunning moment of this play we are safeguarding is repeatable performance to performance while maintaining the illusion of spontaneity. What if you could have a partner who had their eye on that? Not just in the "kissing" scenes, but throughout? What is the role of touch in the play? Of closeness? How is that story being told?

Actors are denied their agency so frequently. They're being told they're lucky to have a job. That sacrifice I spoke of earlier? It applies everywhere. Actors are way too frequently rejected and way too frequently told that there's nine million more of them in line behind them. Actors are taught to be grateful – which is outrageous! Grateful for being excellent at their very own job? I bring this up because actors have been trained into terror about speaking up for fear of losing their jobs. They perform under duress, they perform with loved ones in the hospital, they perform with a stomach flu. Actors can often feel like they don't have autonomy over their bodies and are unable to discuss what they need and want in a space. A space where they are being paid to tell a story using their bodies! And some of that lack of autonomy is out of a power dynamic that feels implicit with their Director. The Director is not only the leader in the room, but also a potential employer in a very competitive industry. There are times an actor can feel "I don't want to speak up. I don't want to be a problem." Bringing in an Intimacy Director creates a neutral third party to relieve the actor of any worry in that regard.

When an actor isn't comfortable with what they're being asked to do – whether with their bodies or intentions – and the history of the American Theatre has told them to "put up and shut up" how will they be able to do their job well with that type of psychological distraction? Don't forget the secret that shall be a secret no longer:

You Need an Intimacy Director.

I recently directed the Kirsten Greenidge play *Our Daughters, Like Pillars* at the Huntington Theatre in Boston, MA. The play is about a Black family, on a summer vacation, hungry to heal their family wounds amongst the hilarity of karaoke and family recipes. There are scenes where characters kiss, where they pursue each other with a sexual hunger. There are scenes where they deeply wound each other as well as scenes where they cling tightly as only family can. I'm a White-presenting Director and know there are some aspects of this play that aren't my story or within my range of lived experience. And then I met, as I call her, Dr. A. And together, our partnership and the collaboration of many others created something quite beautiful.

Together Dr. A and I were able to establish a vocabulary not only for the room, but also for our work on intimate scenes. She leads this fantastic workshop which I recommend for all productions. Dr. A creates a positivity around having agency to speak for what you need without the fear of judgment or retaliation. In it she teaches that "no" is as viable an answer as "yes." A moment I remember so clearly is Dr. A coaching an actor through talking about a recovering arm injury. Eventually the actor landed on "You may touch my arm, gingerly." We all warmed in that moment, leaning into the specificity that Dr. A inspired. In giving instructions on how to better love you, care for you, scene partner with you, you are telling someone they are worthy enough to love you, to care for you, to be your scene partner.

In Dr. Ayshia Mackie-Stephenson's Words:

"I realized that with the intimacy work of *Our Daughters, Like Pillars*, I was creating history: I was showing Black love for the stage. I looked upon the choreography I had done with a new ray of light. For example, characters in the play, Vinnie and Morris, have been married for a long time. In one scene, I choreographed them facing the audience with Morris behind Vinnie, his arms around her. She crossed her arms and reinforced his hold. In another scene, he kissed her on the forehead and she kissed his chin and then playfully tapped it with her index finger. I was choreographing tender scenes in which a Black woman was being caressed and adored. How many times had I seen this Black love outside of this rehearsal

room? I have no memory of it. Moments like this of Black love matter; they increase Black sexual health and integrity; they increase
Black access to human rights."[4]

Intimacy direction is integral and holistic. It's not an addition to a process. A Director modeling behavior that says "Your thoughts, your feelings, your boundaries matter" is so important. Let what is *Big* within us
guide us to a place of bringing an Intimacy Director on board on behalf
of safety, storytelling, and advocacy; let what is *Small* within us guide us
to collaboration and wisdom.
Love,
   Kimberly Senior

and with extra special thanks to Pascale Florestal[5]

Notes

1 https://en.wikipedia.org/wiki/Theatre_director.
2 *The Pocket Pema Chodron*, Shambhala Pocket Classics, pp. 66–67.
3 Anne Carson, *Grief Lessons: Four Plays by Euripides*, NYRB Classics, 16
  Sep. 2008.
4 Dr. Ayshia Mackie-Stephenson, "Confessions of a Black Intimacy
  Director: Black Love and Human Rights." https://howlround.com/
  confessions-black-intimacy-director-black-love-and-human-rights.
5 www.pascaleflorestal.com/.

3

DEFINITIONS

Dr. Ayshia Mackie-Stephenson

Choreography: (one of The Pillars) These are the movements that the intimacy director designs for the actors that speak to the context of the work. For any given scene, the choreography should be repeatable so that actors can feel safe and know what to expect.

Closure: (one of The Pillars) This is an activity that closes the session/ day's work. It tells the actor to leave the work in the room; it is a critical act of self-care.

Communication: (one of The Pillars) It is the process by which human beings create meaning, including verbal and nonverbal language, data, signals, and symbols. This is a process, and there should be continuous and honest communication between the intimacy director, the director, the actors, stage manager, and crew.

Consent: (one of The Pillars) It is the permission for something to take place or agreement to do something. Consent can only come from the

DOI: 10.4324/9781003319399-3

person receiving the action and is not static; it is changeable – it can be given or taken away at any time.

Consent CRISP:[1] It stands for Confident, Reversible, Informed, Specific, and Participatory. In CRISP, Confident replaces Enthusiastic because an actor can be confident and determined about their choice to perform an emotionally difficult scene without being enthusiastic about it. Participatory replaces Freely Given because consent cannot exist when power dynamics are at play. According to Marie Percy in Chapter 10, "there are some important differences between true sexual consent, and consenting to touch in a professional or academic setting as part of a job or class. I also use CRISP for this reason" (see Chapter 10 for more context).

Consent: FRIES:[2] Consent is freely given, Reversible, Informed, Enthusiastic, and Specific. Consent is an agreement to participate in any said activity. The person *receiving* the action must give consent. Consent is a way that we can acknowledge our joys and transform our trauma, listen to each other and respect people's bodies. We can't control our past, but we can create art, we can create a world, with consent where we are allowed to control what happens to our bodies in theatre.

Context: (one of The Pillars) This is the story or narrative being told. The story must be understood, including the circumstances around the intimacy simulation.

Culture: it is the shared patterns and shared behavior and beliefs of a particular group, including age, religion, art. geography.

Gender: gender labels refer to the characteristics of women, men, girls, boys, and non-binary people that are socially constructed. This includes expectations, behaviors, and roles connected to being a woman, man, girl, or boy, as well as relationships with each other.[3]

Human rights: human rights are

> rights inherent to all human beings, regardless of race, sex, nationality, ethnicity, language, religion, or any other status. Human rights include the right to life and liberty, freedom from slavery and torture, freedom of opinion and expression, the right to work and education, and many more. Everyone is entitled to these rights, without discrimination.[4]

Intimacy: in storytelling, this can include incidents of death or mourning, simulated sex, kissing, performance nudity, and other sexual, physical, and emotionally intensive acts of a private and/or sensitive nature.

Intimacy Director vs. Intimacy Coordinators: the Intimacy Director
is a movement professional and an actor advocate. The ID choreo-
graphs simulated intimacy scenes, works as a liaison, and advocates for
actors within live performance (i.e. theatre, dance, etc.), while Intimacy
Coordinators work in film.

Racial Justice: racial justice is the act of naming White supremacy and
supporting Black and BIPOC economic, spiritual and political power.
Someone is either racist or anti-racist. Anti-racism involves an active dedi-
cation to breaking down structures that perpetuate White supremacy.
Racism must be named consistently in order to be dismantled.[5] Anti-racism
is a step towards racial justice. Racial justice is the restorative practice that
recognizes racism, acts to stop it, and uplifts those affected by it. Equity,
diversity, and inclusion reward good intentions, but it's time to take the
next step and embrace anti-racist practice, which focuses on results.[6]

Race: it is a social construction; a race is a categorization of humans
based on shared physical or social qualities into groups generally viewed
as distinct within a given society. There is no scientific basis for race.[7] All
human beings are ancestral to Africa.

Racism: racism is a systematized discrimination or antagonism
directed against people of color based on the belief that Whiteness is
superior. The theatre industrial complex is racist, and racism operates
at every level of the institution of live performance and film. White
supremacy is rampant in theatre from ideas for plays, the stories organizations choose to tell and how they tell it, the system of casting, production, and rehearsal, and who gets acknowledged for what roles. There are
those who may not see where it inherently lies in the system because of
their own privilege: see Chapters 4, 5, and 6 specifically, do a close reading of this text in general, and check out the resources at the end of the
book (Chapter 14) to learn more about how racism operates in theatre
and decide how you can play a role in justice.

Sexual Consent: sexual consent is an agreement to participate in a sexual activity. Without consent, sexual activity (including oral sex, genital
touching, and vaginal or anal penetration) is sexual assault or rape.

Sexuality: sexuality is identity. It is a person's ability to feel or have felt sexual or romantic attraction toward themselves and/or others. Sexual orientation determines whom they do or do not feel sexual or romantic attraction toward. (For more information on this concept and its relationship to race, see Dr. Ayshia's Chapter 4 on race and human rights and/or Charlie Baker's Chapter 7 on genderqueer.)

Simulated Intimacy: there are certainly parallels between theatre and reality. However, it is critical to draw lines between reality and the stage. IDs are in the business of simulating intimacy and crafting intimacy for the stage. At the same time, although intimacy is simulated in intimacy direction, the touch or physical interaction from human to human may be and/or feel real. Even though human to human intimacy is normal and expected and the stories we tell on stage have connections to the real world, drawing the line between reality and the story at hand keeps people safe.

Staged Violence:[8] it is choreography that is set to either the implied or scripted moments of storytelling where one or more characters display use of physical force or power against oneself, another character, a group of characters, or community, that either results in the illusion of injury, death, psychological harm, maldevelopment, or deprivation.

Trauma: it is a person's emotional response to a distressing experience, war, sexual violence, coming out, racism. Few people can go through life without encountering some kind of trauma.

Violence:[9] the intentional use of physical force or power, threatened or actual, against oneself, another person, or against a group or community, that either results in or has a high likelihood of resulting in injury, death, psychological harm, maldevelopment or deprivation.

Notes

1 Intimacy Directors and Coordinators, "Level 1".
2 Teen Alert Program, or TAP808 www.tap808.org/consent Planned Parenthood, "Sexual Consent", www.plannedparenthood.org/learn/relationships/sexual-consent.
3 "Gender and Health," *World Association for Sexual Health*. www.who.int/health-topics/gender#tab=tab_1.

4 "Global Issues: Human Rights." *United Nations*, n.d. www.un.org/en/global-issues/human-rights.

5 Ibram X. Kendi, "Book Talk with Ibram X. Kendi on 'How to Be an Antiracist.'" www.aspeninstitute.org/events/gildenhorn-book-talk-with-ibram-x-kendi/.

6 Nicole Brewer, *Anti-Racist Theatre: A Foundational Course*, November 2020

7 "There Is No Scientific Basis for Race," *National Geographic*. www.nationalgeographic.com/magazine/2018/04/race-genetics-science-africa/.

8 Sheryl Williams, Fight Director

9 World Health Organization, *World Report on Health and Violence*, p. 5. https://apps.who.int/iris/bitstream/handle/10665/42495/9241545615_eng.pdf.

4

INTIMACY DIRECTING, RACE, AND HUMAN RIGHTS

Dr. Ayshia Mackie-Stephenson

"Without sexual rights, [human beings] cannot realize their rights to self-determination and autonomy, nor can they control other aspects of their lives."[1] Intimacy directing is a human rights movement. The history of intimacy directing certainly calls upon this human rights legacy. Intimacy work is inspired by the Me Too Movement, which was created by Black American activist and feminist Tarana Burke.[2] In 2006, Burke began using "me too" to help other women with similar experiences to stand up for themselves and other women began using it to tell their stories. Intimacy direction and coordination are based upon this international movement to end sexual violence against women. Intimacy direction became a way to advocate for women in film and live performance and protect them against sexual assault and violence. I assisted Claire Warden, Intimacy Coordinator/Director and Creative Officer at IDC, in a 2019 Stagesource Intimacy Intensive. As stated in Chapter 1, she said something that stays with me: "actors are human beings." It literally

DOI: 10.4324/9781003319399-4

blew my mind. Of course we know this to be true, but how intentional are teachers, directors, and even actors themselves about our right to our humanity in the work that we do in the theatre? Her statement really influenced my perspective on doing intimacy directing as a way to support the human rights of artists. Intimacy directors are advocates. We advocate for actors; intimacy direction helps directors and actors to tell stories authentically and safely. In this chapter, I will speak to the relationship between intimacy directing, race, and human rights, using my experience with the representation of Black bodies as an example of what's possible.

Black love, Black bodies, and Black sex matter because sexual rights are human rights. Theatre has a White supremacist history of oppressing Black sexuality, and it needs to stop. Black people's sexual rights are affected by the way theatre artists represent Black bodies. Black sexuality is portrayed as moral violation, while White sexuality is portrayed as natural and normal. But the sex and love we see on stage and on the big screen are not natural or "normal;" they are shaped by a White supremacist paradigm that determines how everyone's sexuality gets presented.

Black bodies engaging in Black love is a way to resist that paradigm. Sexuality needs to be reconstructed by theatre artists who use their power to tell stories of Black love and create social change. When it comes to intimacy directing, choreography can celebrate Black love as an act of racial and sexual justice. The history of White supremacy attacking Black sexuality is evident. For Black women – and other women of color – the oppressions of racism and sexism operate simultaneously. Look at the iconic case of Sara Baartman (Venus Hottentot), born in 1789 at the Gamtoos River of the Eastern Cape. She belonged to the cattle-herding Gonaquasub group of the Khoi Khoi.[3] Sara was an African teenager lured to Europe to perform for audiences in 1810. Her genitals and brain were posthumously dissected, pickled, and museumized.[4]

Baartman's story ignited my artist-activist journey. In 2016, wanting to speak to the misinformation about her life and to resist racism and the current-day participation in the oppression of Black bodies, I wrote and directed Venus Hottentot: A Short Play, which premiered at Jewel Box Theatre in New York City. Several historical sources indicate that Baartman refused to show her genitals to the public,[5] so I showed her on stage at the Piccadilly Circus, her arms crossed to protect her vagina from the White man trying to display her labia to the audience. I took the opportunity then to treat Black female bodies with love, care, and compassion, and today, through my work as an intimacy director, that is something I am intentional about.

In our recreations of Black sexuality, artists have the opportunity to reveal what is hidden by White supremacy. Staging sex is not just about making a kiss look real. Stories are pedagogy that tell society what is possible. As cultural theorist Stuart Hall stated and performance studies scholar D. Soyini Madison echoes in Critical Ethnography: Method, Ethics, and Performance, "How people are represented is how they are treated."[6] Baartman's human rights were not only violated in 19th Century Europe – her human rights are also violated by the ways theatre and media remember her and tell her story today. And like the International Women's Health Coalition states, for human beings, "the right to control their own bodies and their sexuality without any form of discrimination, coercion, or violence is critical for their empowerment."[7]

Attempts to control and unfairly represent Black sexuality in theatre and media result in many of the human rights abuses Black people face on a daily basis, including gender-based violence and limitations on our mobility, dress, education, employment, and participation in public life. Because Sara Baartman was lured onstage to perform, other young African women were lured onstage to perform. Attempts to violate Black sexuality in storytelling can also affect the intimate relationships between Black bodies off stage. As one HowlRound audience member stated during the Confessions of a Black Intimacy Director talk, "We don't even know how to touch each other."[8]

When staging Black intimacy, I must be intentional about undoing this harm. In 2020, I started working with Huntington Theatre Company in Boston, creating the intimacy choreography for Our Daughters, Like Pillars, directed by Kimberly Senior and written by Obie Award – winning playwright and Boston native Kirsten Greenidge. Our Daughters, Like Pillars is about Black love. It's about the ties that bind us to our families. Just before the pandemic and my last day in rehearsals, a Black actress pulled me aside and walked me down the hallway. We left the large rehearsal room on the second floor of the Huntington with a calm silence. We found ourselves at a large window in the stairway; she slowed down and turned her body towards me. She was an older woman, the sunlight lit the hundreds of soft wrinkles in her face when she looked into my eyes and spoke, "I've never seen Black bodies loving each other on stage." I bent my head down, thinking neither had I.

It was in this moment with this Black actress that I yearned for Black love and felt such grief for not seeing it on stage or anywhere else. It was in this moment that I wondered how much the stage and media had fueled my own personal disconnect with Black love. A lot of what Americans know about race comes from the stories artists tell. I grew up on the stage and still never saw Black bodies loving, touching, or being tender. And I can recall – as a child and now – the absence of Black love coupled with the atrophying and recycling of the Black man/White woman (or light-skinned/mixed race) romance.

At the stairway, a flood of anger and pain rushed through my body – anger at my father who left when I was an adolescent, anger that Black women are not protected, anger that Black women have to take care of Black men. I recognized my own turbulent relationship with Black love, my focus on Baartman and pain as opposed to love and joy. I recognized my need to see stories of Black love: I need to see us meet, fall in love, and make love. I recognized America's need to see stories of Black love and how much healing that could bring.

I realized that with the intimacy work of *Our Daughters, Like Pillars*, I was creating history: I was showing Black love for the stage. I looked upon the choreography I had done with a new ray of light. For example, characters in the play, Vinnie and Morris, have been married for a long time. In one scene, I choreographed them facing the audience with Morris behind Vinnie, his arms around her (see Figure 4.1 for an example of this choreography, which Dr. Ayshia intimacy directed). She crossed her arms and reinforced his hold.

In another scene, he kissed her on the forehead and she kissed his chin and then playfully tapped it with her index finger. I was choreographing tender scenes in which a Black woman was being caressed and adored. How many times had I seen this Black love outside of this rehearsal room? I have no memory of it. Moments like this of Black love matter; they increase Black sexual health and integrity; they increase Black access to human rights.

Figure 4.1 Nikkole Salter and Postell Pringle in The Huntington's production of *Our Daughters, Like Pillars* by Kirsten Greenidge

Photo: T Charles Erickson.

As the International Women's Health Coalition affirms, sexual rights support the enjoyment of all other human rights and are a condition for equality and justice. As an intimacy director, within the capacity of the play's story, characters, and the intimacy rehearsal process, I have the opportunity to support the human rights of Black actors and encourage their access to these rights. I outline guidance for this in the Exercises section at the end of this chapter. Some of these practices are already basic in intimacy direction; however, it is the intentionality with Black bodies that matters. After that last rehearsal before the pandemic hit, I promised myself to continue building theatre pedagogy on Black love and to be more intentional about Black love when live theatre returns. **With a racial justice intention, intimacy directing can resist White supremacy in the choreography**. Intimacy directors are less likely to commit harm with the intention of advocating for Black sexual and human rights. I will continue to tell the story the playwright and director want to tell, and to tell it in a way that respects the Black actors as human beings who deserve appreciation and autonomy. I will aim to tell stories in ways that allow Black actors to be individuals and not caricatures of racial stereotypes.

I am a sexual being, so, as Gloria Anzaldua states in "Speaking in Tongues: A Letter to Third World Women Writers," I write to "rewrite the stories others have miswritten about me," about Baartman, about Black men and Black women who deserve empowering sexual identities.[9] Sexual rights are human rights, and Black people's sexual rights are impacted by the way theatre portrays Black bodies. Intimacy directors have the choice to decide what their choreography will do – whether it will stand as an act of justice or exploitation.

The theatre world needs to show more Black love, more Black sex, and more appreciation of Black bodies. And the Black love doesn't need to be romantic, it can show sisterhood or other intimate Black relationships (see Figure 4.2 for an example of this choreography between a Black mother and daughter).

Writers must write it, producers must produce it, directors must cast it. And intimacy directors must advocate for it – for Black passion and tenderness, celebrating Black people touching, kissing, and loving one another.

Figure 4.2 Nikkole Salter and Arie Thompson in The Huntington's production of *Our Daughters, Like Pillars* by Kirsten Greenidge

Photo: T Charles Erickson.

Tips & Activities

These tips and activities are intended to be run by the teacher who will need to adjust these exercises depending on their level of experience and expertise. This work supports the human rights of actors and is also useful to theatre artists who are leaders in the room, including the director and/or ID.

1. Questions to Explore in Scene Work

I: Teacher/director − leader in the room. We: Teacher/director and actors ("we" could also include the production team, the leader must set the parameters of "we")

a.   What human rights does this play/scene address (directly or indirectly) and how can I and we support those rights?

b.   How can we focus on the human in the classroom? In the rehearsal process?

c.   How can we subvert White supremacy with the way this scene is choreographed?

d.   How can we support racial justice with the way that we choreograph the Black, indigenous, and/or people of color in this scene? What about with the White characters in the scene?

e.   How can we subvert homophobia and sexism with the way we choreograph this scene?

f.   How can we support gender justice with the way we choreograph the LGBTQ+ and/or non-binary community?

g.   Make sure to ask the actors what they need. This is very important!! What would feel good in this scene for them?

h.   Take the time to address privilege and power: what are the power dynamics in the scene? In the room? In people's lives? Learn and use a map for helping students to identify, support and/or resist difference forms of power in multiple contexts.[10]

i.   How can a student separate themselves from the character? Where are the moments of joy in the room (outside of the scene work, for example)? If it is a racially or gender traumatic scene/play, make sure to discuss with all students how White supremacist and sexist violence impacts us all and offer ways for them to separate the character from themselves. Make sure to have fun and offer opportunities for students/actors to experience joy in the room. "Tapping out" (see Chapter 5, 10, and/or 11 [for virtual examples]) is especially important to this process of helping students/actors to leave the work in the room.

*These questions could also be used to help the teacher access what it is the room and the work needs, and this information can inform what the teacher asks of the ID.

2. *Things To Do (Provide Human Rights Access to Actors by Providing)*

a. **Information and education.** Let actors know who you are (teacher, ID, visiting artist, etc.) and what your role is. Also, let them know what their rights are as students, actors, etc. (*Article 26: Everyone has the right to education . . .*)[11]

b. **Freedom of opinion and expression**. See what the actors do in the scene first and then build the choreography from movements that come naturally to them. (*Article 19: Everyone has the right to freedom of opinion and expression . . .*)

c. **The right to privacy.** I do consent work and check ins regularly, which are critical, because the right to privacy should help the actors protect their bodies and past traumas. I also meet with each of the actors who are in an intimate scene to hear any anxieties or concerns about the scene and allow them to share any confidential information they may not want to share with the cast/crew. Encourage your ID to do this with each of your actors. (*Article 12: No one shall be subjected to arbitrary interference with his privacy, family, home or correspondence, nor to attacks upon his honour and reputation . . .*)

d. **The right to be free from torture or to cruel, inhumane, or degrading treatment or punishment.** I ensure actors are versed with the concept of a safe word, which, when used, stops the rehearsal in its tracks. Consent is fluid, so the actor is never judged or blamed for this. I make sure the choreography is repeatable and that actors know what to expect so that even if the character is being degraded, the actor is not. (*Article 5: No one shall be subjected to torture or to cruel, inhuman or degrading treatment or punishment.*)

e. **The right for their sexuality to be fairly represented.**

    i.   When choreographing a scene between a Black couple, if it fits the story, I like to incorporate gentle touching between the characters. This tender side of Black love is rarely seen on stage.

    ii. Cast dark-skinned Black women in leading roles where they are the love interests and not the "whore," "side-chick" or otherwise "promiscuous" female character in the play.

    iii. Cast Black men actors to play love scenes with dark-skinned Black women.

    iv. Advocate for plays to be used in your department/school that acknowledge and celebrate Black love.

(According to the World Association for Sexual Health, sexual rights underpin the enjoyment of all other human rights and are a prerequisite for equality and justice.[12] For example: Article 5: No one shall be subjected to torture or to cruel, inhuman or degrading treatment or punishment. . . . Article 12: No one shall be subjected to arbitrary interference with his privacy, family, home or correspondence, nor to attacks upon his honour and reputation. . . . Article 19: Everyone has the right to freedom of opinion and expression. . . .)

3. Ubuntu Healing Circle Activity (Grounding Practice That is Based in Human Rights)

*This activity works great with some west African meditation music in the background.

a. Someone says, someone repeats: "Ubuntu means 'I am because we are.' Repeat after me: 'I am because we are'"

b. Someone says, someone repeats: "Ubuntu requires that we are there for each other, supporting and celebrating each other." (voices over each other and lagging is totally fine.)

c. Someone says, someone repeats: "Ubuntu is seen as a traditional African concept."

d. Someone says: "In Zulu culture to greet each other they say: Sawubona = 'We see you', and they respond: Sikona = 'I am here.'"

e. Someone says: "When I say I see you, please respond, I am here. I see you" Group: "I am here"

f. The leader can take the time to repeat this individually. One person in the circle looks at another and says, for example, "Dr. Ayshia, I see you." and then Dr. Ayshia makes eye contact with the person who sees her and says, "I am here." Dr. Ayshia would then make eye contact with someone else in the circle and say their name + "I see you" and the activity continues.

g. Closing practice: resume the circle and everyone closes their eyes to breathe together. Anyone can offer one word at a time into the space before the leader says "Thank yourself for being here and showing up, have a beautiful day, and open your eyes when you are ready."

4. Group Tap In/Out

a. Together in a circle, observe the circle, move together as an ensemble, raise both index fingers up for Count 1, pause fingers around head level and inhale together

b. Keep index fingers up and raise a second finger (like peace sign), clap and exhale together

5. Human Needs Check-In

a. Group: actors (and cast) gather around in a circle.

    i. Director: what are your needs? (*can add "today" for daily check-ins, this is encouraged*)

    ii. Actor A to entire group: (1) "I need you to . . . (listen) (I need you to call me "they") ("I need you not to bring up violence against Black bodies)." (2) Are there any questions? (*The group should ask comprehension questions if necessary, NOT questions that challenge.*) 3) Please raise your hand (or any other gesture) if you agree to respect my needs, thank you.

b. Partners: what are your needs today?

    i. Actor A: what are your needs? (*can add "today" for daily check-ins*)

    ii. Actor B: (1) "I need you to . . . (touch my gently in our scene today) (make eye contact when we pass each other) (I need you to call me "they") ("I need you not to bring up violence against

Black bodies)." (2) Do you have any questions? (*The partner should ask comprehension questions if necessary, NOT questions that challenge.*)

iii. Actor A: I agree to make eye contact with you when we pass each other.

What happens when there is injury? There is bound to be. Check in again about needs. Explore/question where the injury came from, why it occurred and how to stop it from occurring again.

Notes

1 "Declaration of Sexual Rights." *World Association for Sexual Health.* https://worldsexualhealth.net/wp-content/uploads/2013/08/Declaration-of-Sexual-Rights-2014-plain-text.pdf.

2 "Tarana Burke Founder." *Me Too.* https://metoomvmt.org/get-to-know-us/tarana-burke-founder/.

3 See "Sara 'Saartjie' Baartman." *South African History Online.* www.sahistory.org.za/people/sara-saartjie-baartman.

4 See C. E. Henderson. "AKA: Sarah Baartman, The Hottentot Venus, and Black women's Identity."

5 "Sara 'Saartjie' Baartman" Ibid.

6 See D. Soyini Madison, *Critical Ethnography: Method, Ethics, and Performance*, p. 5.

7 YSAFE's "Core Guiding Principles of Working with Sexual and Gender-based Violence."

8 Dr. Ayshia Mackie-Stephenson's talk on *HowlroundTV*, "Confessions of a Black Intimacy Director with Dr. Ayshia."

9 "Speaking in Tongues: A Letter to Third World Women Writers." *Moraga and Anzaldúa*, 1981, p. 169. C. Moraga and G. Anzaldúa, *This Bridge Called My Back: Writings by Radical Women of Color.* Watertown, MA: Persephone Press, 1981.

10 To learn more about power, check out "The bases of social power" by John French and Bertram H. Raven, www.researchgate.net/publication/215915730_The_bases_of_social_power

11 "Universal Declaration of Human Rights." *United Nations.* www.un.org/en/about-us/universal-declaration-of-human-rights.

12 "Declaration of Sexual Rights." *World Association for Sexual Health.* https://worldsexualhealth.net/wp-content/uploads/2013/08/Declaration-of-Sexual-Rights-2014-plain-text.pdf.

5

WHAT THE STUDENT OF COLOR ACTOR NEEDS IN INTIMACY WORK

Sabine Denise

Over the past couple of years, I have become extremely aware of how I feel in my Black body when in spaces occupied by Whiteness. I've found myself questioning whether I belong, I've experienced imposter syndrome, I've felt isolated and invalidated, and I've wondered what biases are being projected onto me. I have questioned whether my ways of being and existing in the world, which are deeply rooted in Black liberation, are important or valid. These feelings stem from the way oppression exists and operates within the body. Oppression persists on four levels: ideological, institutional, interpersonal, and individual – and it all runs deep. The emotional weight and heaviness of having to navigate oppression impacts how I feel internally and the ways I show up in White-dominant spaces. As a young first generation, Haitian-American Black woman, I have grown up breathing in the fog of White dominant culture and racism. I have internalized messages, pseudo histories, and stereotypes about my gender, race, and age. I have carried these messages

DOI: 10.4324/9781003319399-5

in my body for most of my life, and I bring these experiences into every space I enter.

The everyday realities of racial violence and inequities are always present for me. The ways Black women are seen and portrayed in the media and everyday life are things that I carry with me on a daily basis. I have experienced being oversexualized, have had my hair and body touched without my consent, and have had to put Whiteness and its feelings first when speaking about my lived experiences as a Black woman in White-dominated spaces like PWIs and theaters; it's exhausting. As a Black woman, a student at a predominantly White institution (PWI), and an actor, it is important for me to be in spaces where I feel truly seen, heard, and have a sense of agency over my body and choices. As a student actor and person who has been placed on the margins for almost all of my life because of the identities I hold, I know how transformative and healing a space where I am valued and respected can feel.

My need for feeling a sense of agency as an actor is especially heightened when put in spaces where I am asked to engage intimately with people I don't know. When I think of my experiences with and without intimacy directing, I am reminded of the importance of intentionality, socio-political awareness, and racial healing. In this chapter, I will speak to my experiences in theater spaces where my director has and has not had intimacy training, share the exercises used to build trust and intimacy in the rehearsal process, along with recommendations to support BIPOC student actors.

In the summer of 2019, I was invited to play the role of Tammy in *Touching Myself: An Ode to Audre Lorde*, a play rooted in the Black feminist belief that the erotic has the power to guide the fullness we want to experience in every part of our lives. When I think of this play, I am reminded of Audre Lorde's description of the erotic. She states, "the erotic is a resource within each of us that lies in a deeply female and spiritual plane, firmly rooted in the power of our unexpressed or unrecognized feelings."[1] In this play, Tammy and Cindy are two women who see the possibility of the erotic as power when they look at each other, but amidst a climate of racial injustice and bigotry, one of them feels safer in the world than the other. Throughout the play, the two characters share moments of intimacy involving touching, moments of contention related to race and ethnicity, and moments of full pleasure.

My scene partner for the show was a cis-hetero White woman I had never met nor worked with before. I name her identities for two reasons; one being that identities matter. Identities make up who we are, impact the ways we're seen in the world and how we engage interpersonally. My scene partner and I were both cis women, but our individual lived experiences were inextricably linked to our racial identities. Having an intimacy director who is aware of the socio-political realities of how BIPOC and White bodies exist in the world is key to supporting actors in exploring these topics and choreographing the intimacy. The intimacy directors' awareness and commitment to participating in creating spaces for racial justice and healing will support the process for building deeper trust amongst the actors. With this knowledge, the director brings in a deeper level of intentionality that centers the actors' agency and trust.

The second reason I name her identities is because I didn't know her; nor did I trust her. It's important for me to mention that rehearsals for this play took place after my first year of grad school, after having completed a B.A. in African American Studies. I was still in a space of distrust when it came to engaging with White people because of my experiences in school and the content I learned. I lived in a space of suspicion, and I was working to heal from that. During our first rehearsal, I remember being a bit closed off to her. I was aware of the moments in the play that required intimacy and physical touch between the two of us, but this was the first time I remember hoping the director would have a process to help guide us to these moments. There was no existing relationship between her and I, and this was a first for me. I was used to being in plays with the artists in my life, but in this instance, I knew I would need a process and a critically conscious director to help guide the trust needed to fully embody our characters and their relationship.

I found myself hoping for intimacy direction – even though I didn't have the exact name for it at the time – from a director who had a critical and historical understanding of the ways oppression has manifested interpersonally and culturally between Black and White women, understood that the body is political in the ways trauma lives in the body, and saw the importance of healing. When we gathered for our first rehearsal, I remember the director, a Black woman whom I have worked with before and trust, first naming that she was aware of the intimacy involved in this play, and her intentions for making this a process grounded in consent and trust. She let us know that she recently became certified in intimacy pedagogy and choreography. Prior to this experience, I had not worked with a certified intimacy director. She led us through a consensual process of learning and embodying our characters and the essence of their relationship. At the top of every rehearsal, we would first check-in about how we were coming into the space; this allowed for us to share whatever might be getting in the way of us being present with one another. We would then tap-in with each other face-to-face with our palms connecting as we took intentional breaths together. This tap-in was a way of inviting our minds and bodies to be present in this space together. Touch and eye contact are powerful tools that support me in seeing the human before me, remember to hold my judgments softly, and reflect on my own assumptions.

Our director would then follow up with a consent check-in focusing on boundaries connected to our bodies for the day. During these boundary check-ins, my scene partner and I would start by facing each other. One of us would start the check-in by asking the other, "what are your boundaries today?" She or I would then respond with whatever boundary felt important for us to name. For example, there were moments when I wouldn't want her to touch my lower back, and in those moments I would say, "I don't want my lower back touched." Upon hearing that boundary, she then repeated what she heard back to me. For example, she said "What I'm hearing you say is you don't want your lower back touched. I will not touch your lower back." We would then start rehearsing the scenes.

These exercises, along with the intentional conversations we would have about race, class, gender, etc., invited and empowered me to name the ways I wanted others to engage with my body, knowing that each day might be different than the last. I was invited to lean into the process of learning my scene partner and strengthening our connection in order to really lean into play during the rehearsal process. Lastly, the director guided the trust building process with exercises that explicitly invited us to name our boundaries, really see each other, and helped me feel safe enough to let my guard down. I knew that when I walked into the rehearsal room, my needs and boundaries would be respected. I knew I could voice any other boundary as they came up for me. I felt the fullness of my agency when choosing how my body would be in relation to another's. I got to voice how my Black body would show up in this space, and that felt healing. The exercises and director's orientation to the work supported my journey of trust, and ultimately allowed me to show up more fully as myself and the character (see Figure 5.1 for an example of this, when Sabine shows up more fully as herself and her character, Tammy, who is inspired by Audre Lorde).

As I reflect on my first experience with intimacy directing and the process for developing trust amongst actors, I am reminded of experiences with the same intimacy director, but before she was certified in Intimacy Direction. Prior to working on Touching Myself, in the summer of 2018, I had the opportunity to play the lead role in the production of Brooklyn Bedroom, a play that brings you into the everyday life of Tally, a confident

Figure 5.1 Performing Touching Myself by Dr. Ayshia Mackie-Stephenson at DC Black Theatre & Arts Festival with actors Sabine Jacques (left) and Amanda Hurley (right)

Photo credit Dr. Ayshia Mackie-Stephenson.

Figure 5.2 Performing Brooklyn Bedroom by Dr. Ayshia Mackie-Stephenson at Umass
          Amherst with actors Callum LaFrance (left) and Sabine Jacques (right)
Photo credit by Brian Moore-Ward.

and sexually liberated Jamaican-American woman, and the relationships
between her family and romantic partners. In the play, Tally's love interest, Eric, is played by a friend of mine who identifies as a cis White man.
We are introduced to Tally and Eric's love story as we learn of Tally's
journey in embracing the erotic as power in all of her relationships (e.g.
romantic and familial). As we move through the play, we see a number of
moments where Tally and Eric are emotionally intimate, engage in physical touch, and exchange bodily fluids through kissing (see Figure 5.2 for
an example of how Tally (Sabine Jacques) and Eric (Callum LaFrance) are
emotionally intimate and engaged in physical touch before kissing).

There are also moments in the play when Tally is engaging in physical
touch via massaging with her client Mike, while wearing lingerie. Before
taking on the role of Tally, I hadn't been in a play that involved so much
intimacy between actors. This was all very new to me at the time.

As a way to support the intimacy required between Tally and Eric, the
director would invite my scene partner and I to engage in exercises that

were meant to foster a deeper sense of trust and connection. During one exercise, my scene partner and I were asked to go into a separate room alone and to massage each other's shoulders while asking each other questions. Because I had a previously established relationship with my scene partner, I didn't question the exercise. He was someone I knew, had engaged in dialogue about race and gender, and trusted. Whilst this was the case in this instance, I know that I would have felt uncomfortable engaging in this exercise with someone I didn't know. I would not have felt safe being in a room alone with another White man or any actor I didn't know because of the lack of trust. And as I think about this further, I'm not sure I would have felt comfortable voicing that concern without fear of being seen as difficult or the worry that the director would not want to work with me again.

This worry became a bit more present for me when rehearsing and performing the scenes when my character Tally has to give her client a massage. When rehearsing this scene, the director would lead my scene partner and I through a general check-in (e.g. how are you? Do you feel okay doing this?), but did not follow up with more. Unlike my experiences in Touching Myself in 2019, the director did not have us tap-in nor provide boundary check-ins. At the moment, I didn't say anything or think too much of this because the rest of the cast were close friends of mine, and I felt comfortable rehearsing this scene knowing they were around. As I reflect on this experience, I'm able to see the moments when my own internalized oppression was present in the rehearsal process due to the lack of agency and comfort I felt. I didn't feel like I could voice what was happening for me internally because of internalized fears of how I would be received and/or perceived. In the long run, I would have preferred if the director brought in an intimacy coach or would have facilitated the trust building process with more intentionality.

Intimacy work rooted in racial justice and human rights provides space for BIPOC student actors to feel affirmed in the rehearsal space. This kind of intimacy work supports creating spaces where BIPOC student actors feel like their lived experiences are valued, understood, and their agency is centered. The practices included in intimacy coaching and direction are ones that disrupt White dominant norms of urgency and sticking with the status quo. Intimacy coaching practices invite us to see the full humanity of ourselves and each other, while also inviting us to lean into our agency to create safer spaces that speak to how we want to engage and be engaged with.

Tips and Activities

These tips and activities are intended to help the teacher with intimacy and trust building.

1. Tap In & Tap Out

a. Put in Partners
b. Partners face each other
c. Partners inhale and lift both palms up
d. Partners connect/tap their palms and exhale (repeat)
    i. <u>Purpose: connect and establish trust: which pillars at work?: Communication & Consent[2]</u>
    ii. <u>When to use: at the top of rehearsal/before intimacy and after</u>

2. Check-In Prompts

a. Check-in prompts invite artists to share candidly about what is happening in their lives. This moment of sharing allows for artists to clear their minds of whatever might be stopping them from being present or at least gives them the space to name it, even if it's not always possible for them to stop thinking about it. It also gives actors the opportunity to share about the good they've experienced as well.
    i.   What has it been like to be you lately?
    ii. What is your internal weather report coming into rehearsal? (i.e. I feel sunny. I feel like a light sun shower.)
    iii. Name one moment of joy from the week.
    iii. What is one thing you are proud of?

Check in: boundaries: no buttocks, genitals, breasts, or any other body part w/o consent, choreography, or conversation.

a. Partners face each other: A: "What are your boundaries today?" B: "I don't want to be touched in basic areas, like my butt, genitals, or breasts. And I don't want my face touched" A: "X, I'm hearing that you don't want your face touched, I will not touch your face." Repeat for both partners.[3]

   i.   Purpose: to establish physical boundaries
   ii.   When to use: after Check-in and before intimacy work

3. Community Practices

a.   Take the time to ground community practices in the rehearsal space. I say community practices rather than guidelines or agreements because it asks that we actively practice how we want to be in spaces with one another and ourselves. This quick exercise and mini dialogue is one that can support actors in creating the foundations for the space they want to be in. These practices can then be brought into each rehearsal space. Each actor can choose one they'd like to focus on for themselves as an area of growth.

   i.   Ex. Make eye contact, practice gratitude for self and others, call-in vs call-out, etc.

4. Play

a.   At the beginning of your rehearsals, take some time to play at least one theatre game as a way to support building trust amongst the actors. Play is key to building relationships because it asks us to tap into our childlike spirits with each other. Try this activity:

   i.   Body Pose Pass: everyone stands in a circle. Person A makes an all body pose. The bigger the better. Person B imitates the pose as closely as possible to the original. Once they do that, they turn to Person C and do their own pose. C imitates the pose as closely as possible to the original. Coach students to move quickly from pose to pose. Don't think about what you're going to do, just make an offer. Don't think about how you're going to imitate the pose, accept the offer and go for it. Once everyone has gone, repeat the exercise, adding in a sound with the pose.[4]

   ii.   Pass the Dance: this game works similarly to the aforementioned activity. Put on upbeat music. Person A does a dance and the entire circle does it too. Then Person B (the next in the circle) goes and the activity continues until the song is over. This is also great for getting students ready for scene work that involves a lot of movement.[5]

Notes

1 Audre Lorde, *Sister Outsider: Essays & Speeches by Audre Lorde*, p. 53.
2 I got these exercises from Dr. Ayshia Mackie-Stephenson. I was an actor in *Touching Myself*, where she used these activities.
3 I got these exercises from Dr. Ayshia Mackie-Stephenson. I was an actor in *Touching Myself*, where she used these activities.
4 Linsay Price, "Devising Exercises for the Drama Classroom," *Theatre Folk.* www.theatrefolk.com/blog/devising-exercises-for-the-drama-classroom/
5 This activity is from Dr. Ayshia Mackie-Stephenson.

6

YOU CAN'T COLORBLIND CHOREOGRAPH

THE IMPORTANCE OF CULTURAL COMPETENCY IN INTIMACY PRACTICE

Kaja Dunn

Performed intimacy often refers to the physical: staged sexual content, intimate physical contact, nudity or partial nudity, and sexual violence. In addition to the content of sexual nature, intimacy may also include content that encompasses identity, things like race, disability, religion, age, or other heightened personal experiences with appropriate cultural context and competency.[1] These are acts of intimacy that exist in a deeply cultural context. There is still much to be explored in the applications of their theories and words to the practice of staged intimacy (choreography, coordination, and direction) and how it can impact the performance of intimacy on stage and screen. At the heart of it, the negotiations we engage in as people, particularly marginalized people, must navigate both our own multiple histories and the complexity of the "outside gaze." These complexities mean that to choreograph bodies in both intra and interracial scenes takes nuance and an understanding of

DOI: 10.4324/9781003319399-6

theories around race and sex and history of the people involved, both as participants and as observers.

We Aren't Starting With a Black Slate

Sex and sexuality are inherently tied to identity (see Chapter 3 Definitions). The ability to institute cultural competency into intimacy coordination is vital for many reasons. Whether one discusses it or not, race affects perception. As Michael Apple stated,

> It would not be possible to fully understand the history, current status, and the multiple effects of current . . . policy in either the UK or the US without placing 'race' as a core element of one's analysis. Race is a social construction. . . . Race may function as an absent presence in discussions of markets and standards.[2]

The rise of intimacy professionals on set and in the rehearsal room correlated with awareness of the "Me Too" movement and the abuses that were taking place in the entertainment field. But much like the media erased the Black Woman origins of the "Me Too" movement, (Tarana Burke founded the #MeToo movement that gave intimacy its promi-nence).[3] The field of intimacy practitioner work at its inception also over-looked that many of the ideas around consent and boundaries on which the field is based, comes from the generations of work done by Black feminist scholars like Audre Lorde, bell hooks, Tarana Burke, and others. This ignorance allowed (mostly) White women to shape and profit from intimacy work while interested practitioners of color found themselves excluded from the field by its content, structure, and cost. Sometimes in the rush to "claim innovation," harmful practices were actively being enacted which led to both willful and unintentional exclusion in the room. While some practitioners have openly acknowledged that no one person created the idea of consent or boundaries, and that the practical application is built on practices seen in many theatre communities of color, others have insisted on "ownership."

In response to a lack of diversity in early cohorts of classes in July of 2019, Laura Rikard and Chelsea Pace of Theatrical Intimacy Education reached out to me to consult on developing a scholarship to increase diversity in their training. My question to them was "What are you offering in terms of content that would interest practitioners of color?" They asked if I would utilize my work in cultural competency and apply it to the field of intimacy. Thus, a partnership and the development of the first classes contacting cultural competency and intimacy were born.

As a theatre teacher, I had been incorporating a consent and "right to say no" clause in my syllabi as early as 2012. At the time, some other actor trainers thought I created an unprofessional environment when I informed students, they had a "right to say no" to material and that they should have ownership of their bodies. This desire and awareness came from my positionality and awareness as a Black woman who had gone through three conservatory programs, often being "oversexualized" because (in the words of my first undergrad acting instructor as he made reference to *Monster's Ball*): "These were the roles you can expect to play."

In discussion with both concerned IC (intimacy choreographer) practitioners and other educators and tastemakers, it became clear that much of the work around intimacy focused on a gendered and sexuality binary without regard to the very large role racial hierarchies play in power and consent. **Race affects power and consent dynamics.** To fully advocate and help bring about a culture of consent and boundaries, one must understand how these dynamics are at play in the room due to

- History of colonization and sex
- Hidden White woman power dynamics
- Scarcity
- Perceived power
- False universal standards

There were other choreographers in the field who were also thinking about the ways in which the work wasn't completely addressing their experiences or concerned about the ways in which racial, cultural and identity boundaries and consent and cultural competency were not being factored into training. As I developed classes on race and intimacy, they developed companies focused on this work: people like Ann James of Intimacy Coordinators of Colors in the US, Michela

Carattini of Key Intimate scenes in Australia. Sasha Smith and Teniece Divya Johnson appeared in *Elle* highlighting their work as Black Intimacy Coordinators.[4] A few years into my work and the work of others in the field and after a forced "racial reckoning in 2020," there is more awareness of the importance of identity in the shaping of intimate stories, but when I began the need was clear to articulate the concept of racial identity affecting consent. Even today, people, including theatre makers, can confuse diversity with lived representation while ignoring the deep scholarship around racial tropes and sexualization.

So why is it so important to incorporate an understanding of the role race, culture, and colonization have on race and intimacy? There are many reasons. The first is: race is misunderstood. By its nature and structure, race is not stagnant, biological, or easily defined. Winant and Omi in *Racial Formation in the United States* describe race as "an unstable and 'decentered' complex of social meanings constantly being transformed by political struggle," and that "ace is a concept which signifies and symbolizes social conflicts and interests by referring to different types of human bodies."[5] Alan Goodman, professor of biological anthropology, says "race is rather an idea that we ascribe to biology."[6] These nuanced definitions give a starting place to a question many folks struggle with, when I ask it in a *Foundations of Race and Intimacy* class, which is: "what is race?" The answer is elusive and that is by design.

> When European explorers in the New World "discovered" people who looked different than themselves, these "natives" challenged then existing conceptions of the origins of the human species . . . Europeans wondered if the natives of the New World were indeed human beings with redeemable souls. At stake were not only the prospects for conversion, but the types of treatment to be accorded them. The expropriation of property, the denial of political rights, the introduction of slavery and other forms of coercive labor, as well as outright extermination, all presupposed a worldview which distinguished Europeans – children of God, human beings, etc. – from "others." Such a worldview was needed to explain why some should be "free" and others enslaved, why some had rights to land and property while others did not. Race, and the interpretation of racial differences, was a central factor in that worldview.[7]

Europeans put themselves at the center of what it meant to be human and (to their perception), the less one was like them, the further down the hierarchy they were. Europeans developed false scientific taxonomic categories. Much like the way they traveled the world describing trees and birds, they also developed categories of humankind, and racial tropes and stereotypes became central to these classifications.

As addressed by Winant and Omi, racial definitions are not stagnant. Nor are they clear; if you read the Webster Dictionary definition of race up until 2021, it reads:

race noun (2): definition of race (Entry 3 of 3)

1: a breeding stock of animals
2a: a family, tribe, people, or nation belonging to the same stock
2b: a class or kind of people unified by shared interests, habits, or characteristics
3a: an actually or potentially interbreeding group within a species
also: a taxonomic category (such as a subspecies) representing such a group
3b: BREED
3c: a category of humankind that shares certain distinctive physical traits

4 obsolete: inherited temperament or disposition
5: distinctive flavor, taste, or strength (Merriam-Webster)

These entries highlight the through line of "breeding" and "stock". The very formation of race as a construct is tied to the way Western colonization developed.

Intimacy and Sex Are Both Shaped by Cultural and Supremacy Stories

Race and culture impact intimacy just like they impact every area of our lives. While sex differences are rooted in biology, how we come to understand and perform gender is based on culture (see Chapter 3 Definitions). We view culture "as a process through which people circulate and struggle over the meanings of our social experiences, social relations, and therefore, ourselves."[8] If we accept the premise that how we perform gender and/or sex roles is based on culture, we must also embrace the notion that intimacy is deeply cultural. In addition, Whiteness is viewed by theatre and film makers historically with a false universality.

> Race as a category is usually applied to "nonwhite" peoples. White people usually are not seen and named. They are centered as the human norm. "Others" are raced; "we" are just people . . . the idea of whiteness as neutrality, as that which is not there, is ideally suited for designating that social group that is to be taken as the "human ordinary".[9]

This false universality leads to a bias in standards about how intimacy is perceived and translated in story on stage and in film. It can also lead to the disenfranchisement of intimacy professionals from global majority (people from Black, Indigenous, Latino/Latinx, Middle Eastern, and Asian) backgrounds. White IC's are often seen as fit to do *every show* while the global majority Intimacy professionals is either ignored or only sought to do shows in which they share a cultural identity. In addition, practitioners of color can be relegated to emerging roles or only being accepted if they follow Euro-Centric practices. There is often unchallenged bias as to who is put forth to be expert and who leads conversations in the room. It means that othered views of cultural intimacy can often prevail, "The power of the colonizer is fundamentally constituted by the power to speak for and to represent."[10] This construct becomes even more problematic as we see the profession spread to countries throughout the global south while deploying a Euro-Centric lens, certification, and praxis.

The stereotypes developed during the time of colonization still appear as tropes on stage and media. The idea of the "Fiery Latina," a Black woman as an "Oversexed Jezebel," the sexually docile Asian Man, and so many other tropes have been reinforced now through centuries of storytelling.[11,12] These stories allow for a diminished view and ingrain suppositions and biases around behavior, ideals, and sexuality. They also can create unconscious biases about truth in storytelling, who needs protection, who is fragile, and what looks "natural."

Much of the work around racial/sexual tropes originated with Black Feminist thought, as did many of the elements on which the practice of intimacy is based. Intimacy practitioners laid the premise and foundation of their field on the works of such scholars as bell hooks, Audre Lorde, Patricia Hill Collins, Kimberlé Crenshaw, Francis Beale, Angela Davis, Paula Giddings, Alice Walker, and practitioner/scholars such as Dr. Lisa B Thompson and Dr. Barbara Ann Teer (among so many others). Intimacy practitioners laid the premise and foundation of their field on the theories around consent, Queer theory, boundaries, harm, care, intersectional identities, and researching and theorizing tropes. Moreover, because of the harm caused in so many storytelling spaces, Black and other Global Majority directors have often utilized many tools (such as de-rolling and consent and care) in their rehearsal rooms. Some of these directors have pushed back against the idea that this field and approach are "new." This is the case especially when coordinators are not incorporating identity and culture into their work and analysis or thinking about how Black and other Global Majority directors have been historically disenfranchised.

By the same token, certain gestures and acts of intimacy are culturally specific and unique.

> The basic conclusion was that love is a universal emotion experienced by a majority of people, in various historical eras, and in all the world's cultures, but manifests itself in different ways because culture has been found to have an impact on people's conceptions of love and the way they feel, think, and behave in romantic relationships . . . cultures influence how people feel, think, and behave being in romantic love.[13]

Some examples would include, for example: in the Black diaspora, a man sitting between the legs of a woman having his hair cornrowed; a Cuban friend recalled watching their grandparents dancing in the kitchen together; the way platonic physical touch frequency of male Pakistani friends who have immigrated to Norway has reshaped frequency of touch among native Norwegian men in Oslo.[14] To effectively utilize physical touch in story, one must be able to understand and appreciate both the rich cultural nuances of intimacy and understand sexual bias from supremacy structures.

Race Affects Power Dynamics

One of the most powerful concepts in intimacy work is its recognition that actors are often taught not to say no, and its ability to facilitate pause in the room. Intimacy work recognizes that conservatories and trainers teach actors they cannot say no. In doing so, IC practitioners, when they facilitate a pause in the room, demonstrate the most powerful concept of their work: consent. It can, and often does, fall short when the work fails to acknowledge a power dynamic exists not only between producers and actors, or actors and directors or producers and directors, but in the racial hierarchies that are often at play. Because of the economics of scarcity, power structures, and perceptions, it can be more fraught and riskier for people of color to challenge and speak up in a room. Much research has been done on how people read the bodies and actions of Black men and women. For example, Black and Brown youths' actions are more likely to receive harsher punishment. And what may look like advocacy and speaking up when a White person does it can be read as aggression when it is coming from Black or Brown folks, particularly true as we still see creative and production teams that are majority White for shows that utilize the performances of people of color. Therefore, the prominence of Whiteness in the intimacy field can often conflict with the purpose of creating an environment that incorporates consent.

This is not to say that a White choreographer should never work in a Global Majority show. But it should raise some questions about their prominence, treatment, and monopoly over organizations and training programs, as well as the outsized representation they have in Global Majority works and the number of Global Majority folks who have encountered pushback and hurdles while seeking to enter the field of intimacy. Again, the very idea of the false universality of Whiteness creates a position of privilege and power in the field.

There is no more powerful position than that of being 'just' human. The claim to power is the claim to speak for the commonality of humanity. Raced people can't do that – they can only speak for their race. But, non-raced people can, for they do not represent the interests of a race. The point of seeing the racing of whites is to dislodge them/us from the position of power, with all of the inequities, oppression, privileges, and sufferings in its train, dislodging them/us by undercutting the authority with which they/we speak and act in and on the world.[15]

Hidden White Women Dynamics

History (in the US and elsewhere) is misunderstood and hidden by the same factors of colonization and politics that have influenced other factors of racial inequality. In a field that mainly composed of White women, one of the issues around choreography, boundaries, and consent is that we are not taught complete history. The concept that we need to be aware of is how our bodies are read in the room and make calculations around that is a familiar paradigm to people who hold marginalized identities. People who hold marginalized identities understand the familiar paradigm of how aware they must be of their bodies, how others read them, and the calculations therein. What is much less discussed is the fact that for some people, that White female identity has historically been not just complicit but an active perpetrator in harm. While we may understand modern aggression and the trope of a "Karen," less understood is the role White women played in chattel slavery. In history books, when discussed, the role of the White women is often presented as passively complicit or even as a lesser victim to a White supremacist patriarchy. However, scholars such Stephanie Jones-Rogers, who writes, "White women were key perpetrators in sexual violence against enslaved people. For nourishment of their own children, for profit, for their own will"[16] highlight the very prominent role White women played in perpetrating and upholding the slave trade. One passage of her book cites Henrietta Butler, a formerly enslaved woman whose testimony was documented. She stated:

> *Damn old missis was mean as hell. . . . She made me have a baby by one of demmens on de plantation. De old devil! I gets mad every time I think about it. . . . De baby died, den I had to let dat old devil's baby suck dese same tiddies hanging right here. She was always knocking me around. I worked in the house nursin'.*[17]

In this one passage, we have evidence of a White woman (old missis) who facilitated the sexual assault and forced pregnancy of Ms. Butler, presumably neglected care of the child, forced Ms. Butler into wet nursing her perpetrator's child, and physically assaulted Ms. Butler.

Factoring Race and Identity Into Choreography

The intimacy professional should have an idea of the tropes that exist both presently and historically. Whether the creative team discusses it or not, we have been acculturated into certain character ideas. While I won't expound on them in this chapter, the field of Gender Studies has some extraordinary work on the intersection of race and gender tropes and character types. When possible, knowledge of these can be utilized in the development of choreography.

For example, in the play *Choir Boy*, there are scenes of intimacy between two of the young Black boys in a boarding school (see Figure 6.1 to see Kaja Dunn intimacy choreographing from the floor and developing choreography with Black actors).

Figure 6.1 *Choir Boy* Seattle Co-Production between ACT and The Fifth Theatre
Photo by Gail Benzler.

In choreographing a kiss scene for the piece at the Denver Center, I took into account the White conceptions of Black men as sexually deviant "in all orientations"[18] and the way they also overlook the youth of both Black children and queer children. Taking these factors into consideration, I choreographed a scene involving both loving sensual touch, gestures of consent, and playfulness. This is one example of ways that one can use cultural knowledge and historical understanding to build choreography that challenges dominant tropes and narratives. The combination of applied theory and lived experience becomes a powerful tool for the choreographer with cultural knowledge of the Black American experience. Carlton Molette says,

> Theatre is a reflection of the time, place, and social strata of those who present it and those for whom it is presented. Insights into the artistic creations of a culture are more likely to be valid when they occur after exposure to the values and the dominant creative motifs of that culture. . . . Sensitivity to art is at least as important as knowledge about it. Cognitive learning that begins in late adolescence or later does not produce optimum potential for the development of sensibilities in response to the art of a second culture.[19]

Notice here Molette's emphasis on not just knowledge but a deep engagement with the art and culture to do the work. In the Seattle production later that year, in collaboration with the actor and director, they incorporated an actor's own leg braces and scars into the choreography.

When teaching, I use the example of a box of crayons. There's the basic eight color box, which allows us the ability for some pictures. But how much more exciting was it to get that large one hundred and twenty-eight count box with all of the colors (and the sharpener on the side). A Culturally Competent approach to intimacy allows us to shade our work with nuance, subtitle and creativity in a way that a "color-blind" approach does not. We allow everyone to do their best work.

In order to truly uphold the potential of this field, we must take both the vulnerability of marginalized populations and the exquisite gift of the spectrums of intimacy that cultural competency creates. To not approach this work from both an educated and anti-racist lens builds in some of the same disparities and power structures that the field was created to eliminate. At the end of the day, storytelling shapes culture, and one of the most powerful conduits of storytelling is that of human intimacy. There is an opportunity in the work of intimacy to challenge and celebrate the spectrum of intimacy and tell more truthful stories.

Tips and Activities

1. Tips

a. When choreographing and portraying intimacy/love from groups of marginalized and global majority cultures, choreographers as well as other artists and storytellers (to include directors, filmmakers, producing organizations, playwrights, and others) need to take four things into account:

    i. the difference between intimacy/love and the tensions within the relationship of the partner/partners between their inner intimacy and the outer world,

    ii. history and tropes that shape portrayals of Black love and sex, and how these assumptions and expectations have shaped and limited the role of artists and intimacy professionals, particularly of color,

    iii. how these historical tropes shape audience perception

    iv. actors' boundaries within the portrayal.

*One cannot create a consent-based environment or even choreograph a valid and truthful story without consideration of these factors.

b. In light of systematic inequities, at the very least I believe practitioners must ask "is this my story to tell" and if the answer is that there isn't someone who could be representative to do the work, the next question should be around actions to make sure that people are being identified and brought along. There is no solidarity without sacrifice. However, an increase in diverse contributors to the field benefits everyone.

c. Historically, White women have been able to weaponize their gender. This history does not mean that White choreographers do not engage in the work, but it does mean there is a reckoning due in the way that the field developed and what that means in terms of international codification, certification, and qualification.

- What level of competency needs to exist for someone to be "qualified" in the field?
- In what ways are White choreographers benefitting from "presumed authority" and "belonging" while also utilizing the cultural knowledge and capital of people of color?
- How are the economic structures set up by training and certification programs actively playing into this inequity?

*These are not easy or comfortable questions, but they must be grappled with if we are going to truly create an atmosphere of consent, boundaries, and truthful storytelling.

2. Classroom Exercises

a. Culturally Specific Intimacy

Intimacy can be based in nuanced cultural understanding or in tropes.

Discuss with the class intersectional tropes you may see in the media. Look back 10–20 years; do you see any tropes popping up repeatedly?
Find an article discussing racial/sexual/gender stereotypes in the media, look for an intersectional lens. Have you seen this trope? Where? Is there a show, play, or film that upsets this trope or turns it on its head?
Does your culture or cultures have any culturally specific gestures or acts of intimacy? What are they? What do they remind you of? Can you find any articles or books discussing the things you have observed? Share out or in.

b. Steps to Creating a Culturally Competent Environment

Turn to your neighbors and share specific steps you will take to create a culturally competent environment. When will you do it? How? The more specific the better. If time allows, pick a few, one for 2 days, 2 weeks, and 2 months:

i.   Seeking out resources? For what?
ii.   Practicing challenging bias? How?
iii. Making plans to speak up about a specific problem? When? To whom?
iv.   Making spaces more welcoming? Which ones? How will you do it?

*While the changes may seem small, if everyone works on something big, shifts can happen.

c. Understanding How Whiteness is Centered

i.   What are examples of Whiteness as universality? Some examples might include Band-aids, character shoes, "flesh" colored tights, "Theatre History" meaning a Euro Centric theatre history . . .
ii.   What way do we describe people, things and subjects that are not White?
iii. When Whiteness is centered, how can that create an empathy gap?
iv.   How does this affect society?

Notes

1 Chelsea Pace, et al. give this definition of intimacy in *Staging Sex: Best Practices, Tools, and Techniques for Theatrical Intimacy*.
2 Michael W. Apple, "The Absent Presence of Race in Educational Reform," *Race, Ethnicity and Education*, vol. 2, no. 1, Mar. 1999.
3 Kerri Lee Alexander, "Tarana Burke." www.womenshistory.org/education-resources/biographies/tarana-burke.
4 Candice Fredrick, "What It's Like to Be a Black Intimacy Coordinator in the Era of Consent and Political Resistance." www.elle.com/culture/movies-tv/a33850492/black-intimacy-coordinators-interview/.
5 Michael Omi and Howard Winant, *Racial Formation in the United States*.
6 "Interview with Alan Goodman" in *RACE – The Power of an Illusion: Background Readings*.
7 Michael Omi and Howard Winant, Ibid.

8 Dwight Brooks and Lisa Hébert, "Gender, Race, and Media Representation."

9 Michael W. Apple, Ibid.

10 Marina Heung, "Representing Ourselves: Films and Videos by Asian American/Canadian Women."

11 Bell Hooks, *Outlaw Culture: Resisting Representations*.

12 Dwight Brooks and Lisa Hébert, Ibid.

13 V. Karandashev, "A Cultural Perspective on Romantic Love. Online Readings in Psychology and Culture."

14 Thomas Michael Walle, "Making Places of Intimacy – Ethnicity, Friendship, and Masculinities in Oslo."

15 Richard Dyer, *White: Essays on Race and Culture*.

16 Stephanie E. Jones-Rogers and Allyson Johnson, *They Were Her Property: White Women as Slave Owners in the American South*.

17 Ibid.

18 Dwight Brooks and Lisa Hébert, "Gender, Race, and Media Representation."

19 Carlton W. Molette and Barbara J. Molette, *Black Theatre: Premise and Presentation*.

7

GENDERQUEER INTIMACY

Charlie Baker

Our understanding of gender is constantly evolving, as such the tools and best practices around supporting gender queer performers must also continually grow and change. This is to say this chapter is written with the current best tools available. When better, more specific, and proven effective tools are found, they should be used. The supporting of gender queer bodies in intimacy begins with the examining of "the way things have always been done" and who gets left behind and/or is left vulnerable by those ways.

Seeing the gender binary (two boxes, male and female, with hard lines in between) as a misconception has given way to the developing understanding of gender as a fluid spectrum with "masculine" and "feminine" being two of many umbrella terms for culturally coded behaviors and language. An unfortunate left-over from the gender binary is a linguistic system that erases people that do not identifiably fit into one category or the other. For the purpose of this chapter, it is important to identify what non-binary means in the context of gender.

DOI: 10.4324/9781003319399-7

Non-binary: a gender identity which falls outside of the gender binary, meaning an individual does not identify as strictly female or male. A non-binary person can identify as both or neither male and female, or sometimes one or the other. There are several other terms used to describe gender identities outside of the male and female binary such as genderqueer, gender nonconforming, agender, and bigender. Though these terms have slightly different meanings, they refer to an experience of gender outside of the binary.[1]

Another Important Early Distinction to Make is That Between Gender and Sexuality

Gender is the way a person understands their own identity, especially when considered with reference to social and cultural differences rather than differences in biology. Sexuality is a person's identity in relation to the gender or genders they are attracted to, sexually and/or romantically (see Chapter 3 for more information on these terms).

This distinction is to emphasize that a person's sexual orientation and experience cannot be assumed by the individual's gender. Until recently, stories of intimacy on screen and stage have been largely limited to cisgender individuals, and can often rely on assumptions of what intimacy looks like based on anatomy (i.e. "a person with this type of body always enjoys this type of action and/or stimulation"). Gender inclusivity in intimacy requires an expansive view of what intimacy can look like between humans. A phrase I have often used in rehearsal processes is "if it feels intimate, it's intimacy," this is in regards to both boundaries and choreography. Touching or referring to areas of the body that have been heavily culturally gendered (hips, chest, butt, etc.) may prove uncomfortable or dysphoric to some, and thus prevent the performer from being able to work in an embodied way.

When every person in the room shares their name and pronouns, it removes unwanted and isolating attention from those in the room that may use unexpected or variant pronouns (like the singular they/them or neo-pronouns like ze/zir). An individual's name on paper, or from previous collaboration, may not reflect the one that is shared into the space to be used, defer to the name that has been given by the individual in the room at that moment.

Profuse apologies and/or pressing forward with the conversation without correction doesn't acknowledge the harm done, and can turn the situation into the individual who was just misgendered now having to console someone who caused harm (accidental or otherwise). Accidents happen, and perfection is not the standard; however, respect is. If purposeful and/or persistent misgendering continues, a private conversation with the individual may be in order.

Language continues to be a powerful tool for inclusivity and support when discussing bodies. In order to keep language about the body specific and inclusive, refer to the musculature and the skeletal system.

If bodily language exists on a spectrum, at one end is comfortable slang: the words we will use with our peers and friends in reference to our own bodies. At the other end of the spectrum, is sterile language that is overly intellectual and prevents embodiment of action. The aim is somewhere in the middle: familiar, comfortable, clinical language. Not every person may refer to their pecs as their "breast," and such language may be very dysphoric, and "swimsuit area" in regards to the groin is non-specific and doesn't acknowledge that swimsuits (like bodies) come in different shapes and sizes, so two people's "swimsuit areas" may not be the same. See Figures 7.2 and 7.3 for diagrams with examples of language about the body based on simple muscle groups. By using language about the body that is approachable, inclusive, and specific, choreography and boundaries can be communicated in universal gender inclusive terms that can help prevent erasure of the identities of those involved in the process.

Along with universal language as a useful tool is the power of choice. True choice consists of: the option to say no free of coercion and/or punishment, privacy, and time for decision making. When decisions are being made about dressing rooms, costume undergarments, and other areas that have been regulated to cisgender norms, privately talk with the individual(s) affected by the decision, and present all options available. Whether this is asking a performer which dressing room they would be most comfortable in and offering a third location if possible/desired or presenting a performer with both masculine and feminine costume pieces to see what supports both the performer and the story being told.

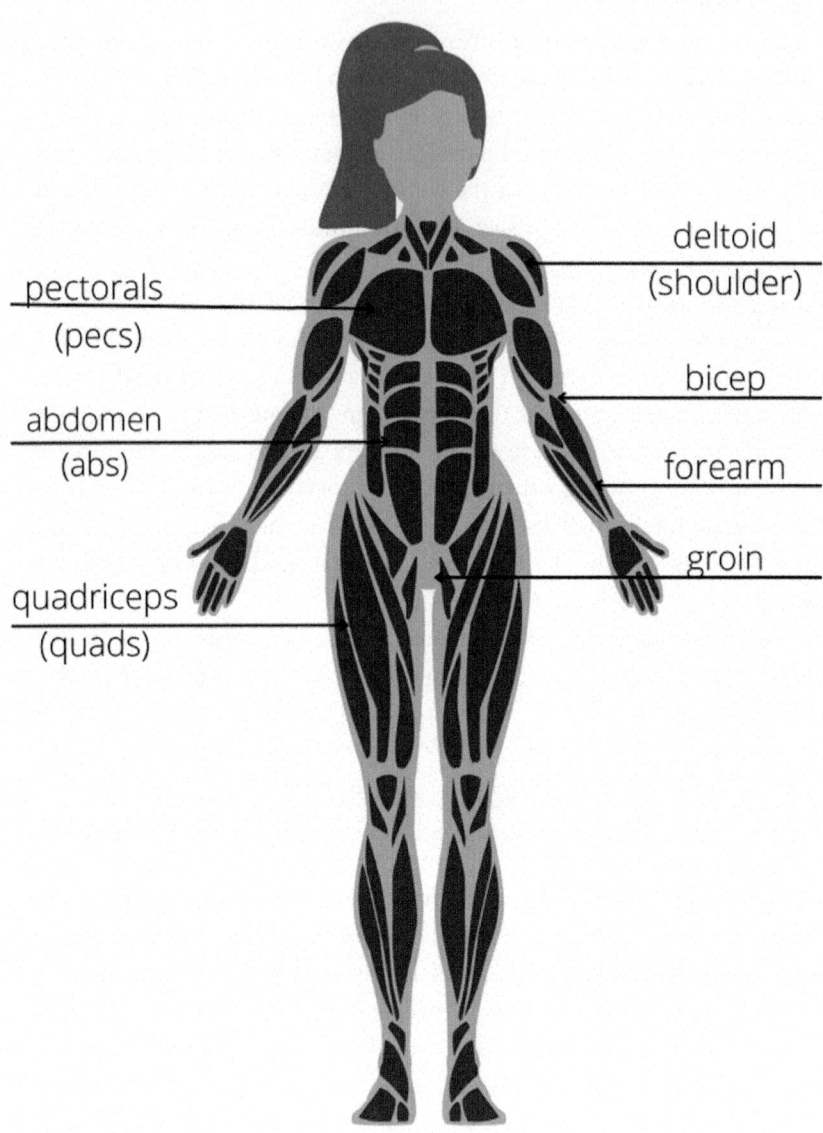

Figure 7.2 Musculature and the skeletal system from the front of the human body, created with stock image by Charlie Baker.

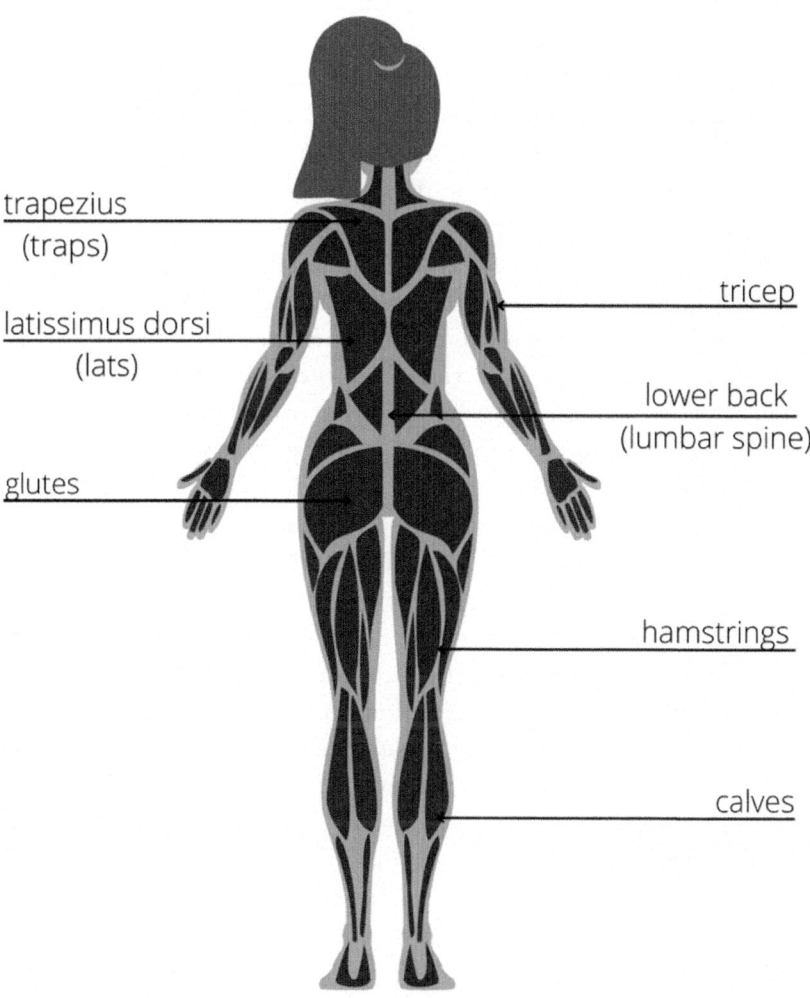

trapezius
(traps)

tricep

latissimus dorsi
(lats)

lower back
(lumbar spine)

glutes

hamstrings

calves

Figure 7.3 Musculature and the skeletal system from the back of the human body,
created with stock image by Charlie Baker.

Inclusive language takes practice. A great exercise to practice awareness of gendered language is to tell a story. It can be a summary of the day or a recent fun event; tell the entire story without use of pronouns (you may or may not decide to include the allowance of "I"). For example, "Charlie, and Charlie's cat stared at the computer screen. While Charlie read the rehearsal report from the day, Taliesin the cat gave a lazy tail flick. The performers had a really great run that evening, the actor playing Troy said that the choreography for the intimacy was comfortable and felt true to story, and Shae, the performer playing Rose, said that tonight felt particularly dropped in." Rewiring language takes time and practice; however, it is important to begin the practice before it is "required" by the presence of a non-binary person.

Advocacy and supporting non-binary performers is a practice in decentering. De-centering is to shift from the established or traditional center of focus – in this regard, it's shifting from the ID (or anyone else in the role of "advocate") to centering the performer who is in need of the advocation.[2] Effort can be required to imagine a genderqueer vision of intimacy; however, the responsibility of the effort cannot be placed on the performer. This would manifest in sentences like "I'm doing my best, but it's hard", "I'm sorry, this is all so new to me." The tools for working with transgender and non-binary performers are new and emerging. It is important to realize that just because they are new to public knowledge does not mean they are new to the world, and often great effort has been made to destroy prior research (i.e. the burning of the Institute of Sexual Research in 1933). When the burden of effort is placed on those who are supposed to be supported by it, the situation flips and now non-binary performers are left to coddle the advocates for their attempts. It is worth reiterating: the standard is not perfection, it is respect. Advocacy begins with de-centering, and asking how the person being advocated for wants to handle the situation. While carrying the banner may feel good, unchecked and unwanted advocacy can put the performer in danger or isolate them from the cast. This would be behavior like loud statements or personal questions made in reference to the individual in front of the cast, or advocating for them in a situation after being asked not to.

Working with transgender and non-binary performers may require some new modes of operating, but a majority of the tools of inclusion are simple: respecting names and pronouns, asking pertinent, but not personal, questions, and being open to using the tools that performers themselves have found useful.[3] Performers have been taught to "tolerate" a lot within performance. However, with proper support, that tolerance can shift into embodied performance.

Tips and Activities

1. Tips to Support Queer Performers

a. When accidental misgendering happens, apologize, correct, and move forward with the interaction using correct pronouns, and gently correct those using the wrong pronouns *without shame*.

   "I was talking to Daniel and he – sorry, they – told me the scene went well!"

   or

   "Have you seen June? They're not in the dressing room."
   "She, June uses she pronouns."
   "Thank you! Have you seen her?"

b. Group addresses are also an opportunity to be inclusive of the group. "Y'all," "folks," "cast and crew," "everyone," etc. are ways to gather attention in the room without resorting to "you guys," "ladies and gentlemen" or other terms that enforce a gender binary.

c. The first useful tool in a rehearsal and/or classroom is language. As instructors and intimacy professionals in the room, it is our opportunity to model language to be used in the room, beginning with introducing oneself to the room with pronouns.

d. Use Figures 7.2 and 7.3 to use inclusive language about the body that is based upon simple muscle groups.

e. If certain costume pieces present issues because of fit or choreography, communicate specifically to the actor what is happening in a way that does not blame the actor's body, and collaborate for solutions.

   "The costume undergarments for this scene are too short for the choreography in this moment, how would you feel about looking at different options, or reexamining the choreography of this scene? We could also incorporate a blanket/the sheets for coverage."

Figure. 7.1 Unseen (2022): Helen Sadler and Nora el Samahy

Photo by Jenny Graham.

Incorporation of the props set around the action (like a blanket) not only grounds the action in the environment but also opens new options to be explored without compromising boundaries (see Figure 7.1 for an example of this: the actor on top is wrapped, shoulder to hip in a brown afghan blanket, and drapes it over their scene partner, covering their torso, in the play "Unseen").

f.   Societal erasure of identity can lead to performers being hesitant to speak up in the room. This is why private check-ins and questions like "may I advocate for you in this situation?" are helpful.

2. Exercises[4]

a. Pronoun Name Game

Instruct the first person to give their pronoun with a descriptor: They Funny. The second person gives the first person's pronoun/descriptor and then their own pronoun/descriptor: They Funny, She Amazing. The third person starts at the beginning, reciting each person before they go and adding her own: They Funny, She Amazing, He Tangy. (Beyond teaching the pronouns in the room, this game is fun and allows actors to build trust. It also allows for inclusivity with cultural language: excluding the verb resists the White supremacy of "formal" English as good and other English as bad. The game shows that all language is good as long as it fits the context.)

b. Gender Inclusive Language Practice

Divide into partners and decide a "partner A" and a "partner B." Partner A will point to a location on their body, making contact (touching the tip of their own nose, grabbing/touching their own wrist, or indicating their collar bone). Partner B will name the part of the body being pointed to, aiming to use clear specific language that is inclusive (i.e. not gendered, or a slang with an extensive cultural context). If partner A believes the word to be non-specific, non-inclusive, or would like partner B to use another term for the same spot, partner A may indicate the same spot again for partner B to pick a new word. ("Scapula" may be specific, but partner A may find the term "shoulder blades" of greater use). If partner A understands the term to be specific and inclusive, they may indicate another part of their own body. After a time, the partners should switch to each get an opportunity to practice naming and specific indication.

Ex: (Partner A lays their hand on their heart.)
Partner B: heart.
(Partner A repeats the gesture)
Partner B: chest.
(Partner A pats their collarbone)
Partner B: clavicle.
(Partner A touches their left pinky) etc.

Notes

1 Madelyn Gelpi, "Best Practices for Non-Binary Inclusion in the Workplace. – Out & Equal."
2 Added by Dr. Ayshia Mackie-Stephenson.

3 Learn more here: www.Xploringgender.com.

4 This activity is the Name Game that was reworked and adapted for gender inclusivity by Dr. Ayshia Mackie-Stephenson. Original game: www.thoughtco.com/ice-breaker-the-name-game-31381.

8

CONSENT CULTURE & DEVISED WORK

Colleen Hughes

The devised theatre rehearsal space is unique. In it, performers are more than interpreters of others' words. They are source creators themselves, coining text, crafting movement, and even making structural choices throughout an extended development process. The resulting performance is one in which their contributions are indelibly molded into the final product.

It is in this setting that I spent many of my early years as a theatre professional. When I began studying to become an intimacy director, many joyfully creative rooms swirled in my mind as I began my work in consent-forward practices. In the course of my time as an actor, I also worked on dozens of productions in the "traditional" regional theatre model: a three-week rehearsal process in which an existing script is efficiently staged and produced. But it was not these processes that were foremost in my mind as I trained in consent and intimacy work. My thoughts went to the numerous physical theatre projects that seemed

DOI: 10.4324/9781003319399-8

to uphold so many of the ideals that intimacy and consent professionals were now working to codify.

What is it about these rehearsal rooms that lifted the human first and foremost? What about the devised process opened the door to the possibility of seeing performers not merely as conduits, but as creators themselves? As I moved from training into practice, I wanted to see what devised work could bring to consent-forward production methodology and in turn discover how consent and intimacy work could further lift the work being done in this subspecialty.

In these pages, I will share what I have learned from both a pedagogical and creative perspective as I have worked to merge these two fields. In my role as Director of Core Training at Intimacy Directors and Coordinators (IDC), I have worked on curriculum for the organization and I am, at the time of this writing, completing preparation for IDC's Consent Forward Artist program. This workshop is a weekend-long in-person program designed for individuals who are looking to better center consent and agency within their spheres of influence in performance and education. I have also taught dozens of classes, workshops, and webinars for IDC as well as for other organizations across the US. As a content contributor for IDC, I have contributed substantially to the online Consent Studio drafting material for educators and entertainment professionals. As an intimacy director, I have worked on productions both in the US and abroad. I have had the pleasure of collaborating on numerous devised projects: dance-theatre, physical theatre, and immersive productions (see Figure 8.1 for an example of me leading a workshop in devising).

It is in these rehearsal and performance spaces that I have really been able to engage with the questions that intrigued me from the beginning of my work with Intimacy Directors International (IDI) in the days before I was part of their first apprenticeship program: what can intimacy professionals and educators learn from the physical theatre spaces that I often experienced as organically validating and humanizing? How can we bring intimacy work into processes in which the content is not predetermined before the first day of rehearsal? In exploring those topics, I have been able to develop a deeper understanding of both of these specialties and the ways in which they can lift each other up.

Figure 8.1 Pictured from left to right: Tessa Kuhn, Hannah Wolff, Colleen Hughes, Elaina Di Monaco, Megan McDermott

Photo by: Rebecca Gudelunas.

Choose the Human Over the Art

One of the dynamics that I was able to identify in many of the devised processes in which I spent much of the first ten years of my professional life, was that in those rooms I was seen as a human first. If I had a flat tire on my bike on the way to the studio, or if my nephew had just learned to walk – these were all experiences that I entered the art-making space WITH. The joys and struggles of life were not distractions to be "left at the door." They were welcomed. I was welcomed, as a whole person, not merely an "instrument." Before beginning to generate new material for the day, or revisiting old material, these rehearsals would often begin with an organic check-in process. Sometimes production ideas would bubble out of these shares, but more often it was simply a way for us to join together as collaborators, to see and be seen by each other. It allowed us to immediately take note of the fact that one collaborator might opt for less physically taxing work that day after staying up much of the night with their newborn. Another might be bursting to share a revelation that they had about a creative stumbling block that they had on the trolley returning home after our last rehearsal. Both of those humans were welcomed into the development process that day, and the reality of their lives outside of the room were never seen as a hindrance to the art-making process. Their lives are what make them the collaborators we were fortunate enough to work with. That welcome with its implicit philosophy that "the you who is here is valuable," made me look forward to devised process rehearsals. I would leave feeling rejuvenated rather than drained. I knew that my ideas, my limitations, my needs, my creative contributions, my joys, and my sorrows would be treated with honor. I was a creator in those spaces and who I am as a person is what allowed me to add to the pieces that we were building together.

At IDC, I have shared with students that one of the core tenets of consent-forward practices requires us to value the human over the art. This is not because art does not matter. To the contrary, art is something that humanity has used since its earliest days to share what it means to exist with others who are sharing this earth with us. But in those days of sharing stories around campfires, art was always in service of humanity.

It lifted up both the teller and the listener. Both had a stronger connection to their culture and community for its telling. This element of art in service of humanity – including the humans who happen to be making it – was something that I experienced as a devisor.

It was in many regional theatre spaces, however, that I begin to experience a gap as a young actor. From my conservatory training through "cattle call" auditions, to the rehearsal rooms themselves, there was often lip service paid to the importance of theatre for humanity, but I sometimes felt as though my own humanity was excluded from that equation. From the implicit and explicit commands that "all good actors say yes" to the culturally accepted idea that "there are hundreds of people who will take your job if you're not willing to do x." I felt a profound difference in the way I was treated when working on a three-week "traditional" scripted rehearsal process as compared to the devised work that I so loved to make. If humanity is central to the reason why we make art, even at the largest institutions, then why are the humans who are using their bodies to help tell a story excluded from that consideration? As Sarah Marshall from the podcast "You're Wrong About" likes to sing to a disarmingly cheerful melody, "it was capitalism all along!"[1]

While the process itself was much of what drew us to devised processes, it was the product that frequently drove the focus of rehearsals in regional theatres. Ironically, the product of the former often far exceeded the product of the latter from the perspective of many critics, audience members, and artists within the community. In this product-delivery paradigm in which time is money, the unique contributions and needs of individual actors were considered a drain on that time-money resource. What was valued as essential in one rehearsal room was shut down as a distraction in another. It is in many of these regional theatre spaces in which ticket sales have overtaken any of the stated goals in their lofty mission statements. Not only were they creating uninspiring and sometimes toxic workspaces for their performers, but their productions suffered as well from a deep loss of the contributions of their often brilliant team members whose humanity was not lifted in the process.

This devised vs standard rehearsal process observation was, of course, not always representative of whether or not a process would be healthful. There are physical theatre companies in which a guru culture has built up around individual artistic directors, creating deeply problematic and disenfranchising creative spaces. Conversely, many small and midsized theatre companies, including Curio Theatre[2] in West Philadelphia, with whom I have worked for many years – have a standard season structure. Yet some, like Curio, prioritize the "human first" theatre culture. They value their company members in a way that is palpable. But these exceptions to the pattern are proof that the positive aspects that I was seeing predominantly in physical theatre was not a given. It required conscientious and ethical leadership within the organization. Curio showed me that a healthful culture COULD exist in a three-week rehearsal process. These dynamics were a choice, whether conscious or not, and art-makers could make shifts within their processes if they wanted to start producing rehearsal spaces that allowed all contributors to find their voice and feel valued for doing so.

Human Over the Art in Intimacy Work

It was with these two very different types of experiences that I came to Intimacy Directors International. As I began my training and self-study, I quickly discovered that intimacy and consent work was about much more than stage kisses. This work was and is about making substantial cultural change within an industry that has been chewing up and spitting out actors since the days in which Hitchcock first referred to them as "cattle."[3] The conversations that were happening first in my community at IDI and then later at IDC made me think deeply about the wide variety of experiences that I had working as a performer, a movement director, and a choreographer. Some spaces treated performers as chess pieces, moving them about the space to satisfy a director's vision. Conversely, Adrienne Mackey of Swim Pony[4] was one of the strongest directors that I have collaborated with. She never treated us as lumps of clay to be molded to her pre-determined shape. Rather Mackey, and others like her, had a level of trust in their own creative offerings as well as that of her collaborators. As such, the material that was generated under her facilitation and direction was unique, specific, unexpected, exciting, and deeply human. The "chess master" directors sometimes made pretty pictures, but the work often fell flat because the performers were not deeply connected to the work.

It was the devised model that most reminded me of the work that we were beginning to do at IDI. When we were training and later as we took on our first productions as apprentices, we never approached our choreography from a top-down position. Consent-forward work was, by definition, collaborative. Our role, as intimacy directors, was to help facilitate that creation process in a manner that reminded everyone that all of us – director, performers, ID – were artists. We had within us, virtually every time, the ability to craft a physical story that served the narrative (and, yes, the director's vision) while honoring the performers' boundaries. The performers were a vital part of the artistic process, generating ideas, learning that their "no" was as welcome in this space as their "yes," and helping to craft a story that they could "live in" during the course of a production. Much like the devised rehearsals in my previous experience, the physical movement crafted in this way was nuanced, unexpected, harrowing, or funny. Intimacy work was putting forth a model of creation that shared DNA with the physical theatre that I so loved. But it was happening beyond the fringe festivals and underground DIY performance spaces. From the time that Alicia Rodis first joined season two of "The Deuce" on HBO in 2017,[5] more than ten years after Tonia Sina first coined the term in her seminal work Intimacy Encounters; Staging Intimacy and Sensuality,[6] it was clear that intimacy work was ready to take on the entertainment industry at its most influential levels. Here was an opportunity to help make much-needed change while working in a manner that deeply resonated with me as an artist – and this team wasn't satisfied to make these shifts on a small scale. Rodis, Sina, Siobhan Richardson, and Claire Warden[7] were taking it to the top and the impact of their work is being felt across the industry and around the world today.

As a physical theatre performer and movement director, I knew that I brought a strong working knowledge of movement as storytelling to the table. But I also learned that there were elements of what would go into this job that went far beyond choreography. Claire Warden had worked closely with a mental health professional learning the ways in which trauma can show up in the body in order to incorporate this understanding into the methodology of the work. I was learning the importance of mitigating harm in order to help facilitate spaces in which individuals could participate in art-making regardless of their trauma history. If this work could only be accessible to the lucky few individuals who never experienced coercion or abuse within or outside of the industry, then it would not be elevating the voices of individuals from whom we most need to hear.

I quickly realized that in order to take on this work in a way that was in alignment with my values and that upheld the serious obligation that we take on when we tell performers that we put ourselves forward to act as their advocate if they so choose. I knew that I needed to understand more about the ways in which individuals respond to trauma and, more importantly, what steps I could take as a facilitator to help craft spaces less likely to cause the kind of harm that has been perpetuated throughout our industry for generations. It was with this mindset that I connected first with trauma-informed yoga practitioners[8] and eventually with the Bartol Foundation's Trauma-Informed Teaching Artist program.[9] From that work, I began to recognize elements from the devising rooms that I found so positive. Adrienne Mackey's casual beginning of rehearsals in which we all gathered in a circle in – director, performers, composers, and other designers – and checked in with each other before diving into the day's work was codified in the methodology that I was learning from the Bartol Foundation. This was not merely a chance for friends and colleagues to chat – it was a chance for individuals to share out where they "were" on a given day. And to have that "location" – tired, excited, inspired, worried – be seen and valued. That our work, which in physical theatre often felt very much more like play, could and should be chosen and led by us. What we generated on a "tired" day is no less valuable than the ways in which we collaborated when our energy was high. This was one of the reasons, I was learning through the Bartol training, that trust grew in those rooms without any need for blindfolded "trust-building" (trust-demanding?) exercises that were so prolific in many of the toxic classrooms and rehearsal spaces of my early career. By this simple act of "checking-in" Adrienne, and other physical theatre companies with similar positive work environments such as Tribe of Fools,[10] set up a space that was "trauma-informed" in a deeply important way.

Another element of this work that I immediately recognized as prolific in physical theatre and less accessible in many commercial companies was the role of transparency. Devised work invites everyone in the creation process to be "in on" the development process. As such, an openness around what the director doesn't know yet is essential. This transparency around where we are as a creative team and where we could potentially go was a living example of this value in action. It also served the dual purpose of setting up a situation in which the director isn't perceived to hold "all the answers." Transparency also allows members of the development team to contribute to possibilities that may never have been dreamed up by only a single artist. I remember working on some projects in which a location for performance was not chosen before the beginning of workshops. If the companies had withheld this from us, it wouldn't have allowed us to literally and figuratively explore our city and find new ways and places to tell a story.

As my work with Bartol paired with my work with IDI, I began to recognize WHY some spaces felt affirming and life-giving and others left me feeling drained and unattached. And while that general divide between devised and commercial was often there, Curio and other "exceptions to the rule" served as proof that any theatre space could be human-first in its approach.

As I made these revelations, I was able to contribute to the conversation about what it means to foster a consent-forward workspace. When IDC offered their first in-person workshop, I was able to see firsthand how I could share these lessons as an instructor. In collaborating with Sasha Smith and building from a robust curriculum built by Warden as well as Dr. Jessica Steinrock and Marie C. Percy, we were able to incorporate the values of trauma-informed practices and collaborative movement creation into consent practices as we worked to refine and define intimacy work.

My overlapping professional points of focus came full circle as I began to pivot back into devised and physical theatre work as a certified intimacy director. What does it mean to bring this practice to a rehearsal space that does not function in a standard three-week rehearsal process? How can performers consent to actions within a performance that is yet-to-be envisioned? Despite the wealth of positive experiences that I had working in these processes in Philadelphia, physical and dance-theatre are certainly not without their gurus and dangerous practices. So, how can consent culture continue to uplift this non-traditional way of developing work without demanding that it be something that it is not – forcing it into a space with more structure and perhaps less of that dynamic that made it feel so affirming for all those years? How can intimacy work lift up devised work just as devised work has lifted up intimacy work?

Through ongoing conversations with dance-theatre organizations large and small as well as work with IDC, I have found tools that serve many of these spaces quite well. As is always the case with works in progress, I hope and expect to have learned and built more a year from now, as well as a decade from now. But as of this writing, I am proud to be able to share some tools that have been adapted from IDI and IDC's intimacy practices specifically for those creating work in devised processes. The goal is to continue what is good and find ways to bring even more agency and healthful practices to the physical theatre world.

Tips and Activities
Devising Tools for Change

The pages hereafter include a collection of tools that I have found to be particularly useful in these processes. Much of this listed is used with permission of IDC from a presentation that I built for them entitled "Cultivating a Culture of Consent in Devised Processes"[11] as well as various other presentations that I created under my own company, Intimacy Dynamics LLC, and have presented to learners around the globe.

Before diving into the toolbox, it is essential to definite terms in order to begin to share a vocabulary across segments of the industry. In my presentation for IDC referenced previously, I answered the following question in a manner that I have since found to be very useful and conscientious when thinking about not just scenes of intimacy but also "a culture of consent" writ large:

What Does a Space Look Like That Fosters a Culture of Consent?

- a space in which the individual agency of every human in the room is held as a core value
- in which active steps are taken to acknowledge and counterbalance power structures and dismantle assumptions, habits, and behaviors that do not support this core value

- in which proactive measures are taken to center the autonomy and consent of artists and audience members that participate in an artistic experience

Transparency is a value that I have already discussed in some detail in this writing. Paired with power dynamics and boundaries, it serves as one of three core principles that can underpin consent-forward processes.

Boundaries, of course, have been part of the marrow of intimacy work since its inception, and we will soon break down the specific ways in which boundaries can still exist with clarity in a devised process. Warden's work with French and Raven's Bases of Power[12] combined with her research into scholars of systemic power such as how Kimberlé Crenshaw has informed much of IDC's curriculum and, in turn, the tools that I itemized hereafter for physical theatre creators. Prior to that list, it is essential to name that, unlike oppressive systems of power that express themselves through actions that uphold White supremacy and other forms of oppression, the types of power that exist in a specific workspace, such as title power and referent power, are not inherently harmful. A producer holds the power to make the final decision as to where a production will be held. This is neither coercive nor problematic. But as I first stated in my presentation entitled "Consent & Communication: Practices for a Stronger Community Theatre Culture":[13]

> "Counterfactual **denial** of power can contribute to a coercive environment that can foster gaslighting and even abuse."
> (This language has now been incorporated into IDC's core training on power dynamics.)[14]

This reality is particularly important for those in devised spaces to reckon with. Unlike regional theatre processes in which most people are uniquely aware of the hierarchy, it is sometimes artists in physical and dance-theatre spaces (often underfunded specialties) who are not always able or willing to recognize their own power within a workspace. As such, they can perpetuate harm by pretending (or even believing themselves) that the workspace is a flat circle of influence. This is almost always not the case. Even in communal artistic groups in which no one holds any title power or non-democratic decision-making power, referent and expert power still play a heavy role in the way in which power affects consent in a room. While we cannot wave a magic wand and make existing power dynamics disappear, we can and should look at HOW power is functioning in our creative spaces and take actions that help make sure that those with the least amount of it are able to express their own needs and boundaries without reprisal or punishment.

1. Tools for engaging honestly with power dynamics in devised processes:
    a. An empowered SM throughout the entire rehearsal process
    b. Elected cast representative
    c. Clear reporting structure
    d. Community agreements
    e. Organizational stance and stated response to bullying and harassment
    f. Anonymous reporting options
    g. A professional rehearsal space when financially feasible. (Even on a next-to-nothing budget, rehearsal in a park may be a better fit from a power-dynamic perspective than a rehearsal in someone's living room.)

As previously discussed, transparency is one of the core tenants of consent-forward work. Devisors may feel at a loss when looking at standard recommendations regarding communication, since their material doesn't EXIST before the first rehearsal process. However, looking to "share what you know when you know it" folks in leadership positions can model a culture of transparency even when the project still has many unknowns.

2. Tools for uplifting transparency in devised processes:
    a. Audition postings with as complete as possible description of the project and what artists may expect.

Examples:

    i.   *"This piece will include scenes with extensive acrobatics. A certified acrobatics instructor (name and link) will be working in collaboration with the choreographer and will be available to work with performers throughout the rehearsal process."*

    ii.   *"Final performance will depict multiple scenes of stylized violence representing the experiences of WWI soldiers."*

    iii.   *"Performance will be immersive. Audience members will not be permitted to touch the performers at any time."*

    iv.   *"Performances will be staged outdoors unless the temperature is below 55 degrees."*

b.   Ongoing, active discussion of project development with the entire team – regular "Brainstorm Sharing Sessions" (*These make sure that all team members are "in on" the latest proposals, even if those ideas were conceived over coffee or beer outside of rehearsal hours.*)

c.   Being in open communication about: "*What story are we telling?*" *and* "*How are we telling it?*"

d.   Clear lines of communications that establish expectations regarding workspace behavior – particularly when devisors have overlapping dual (or multiple) discrete relationships (*i.e.: someone is both an instructor AND a performer, someone is both a mentee AND a director, someone is both a collaborator AND a significant other*). These dynamics, which are prevalent throughout the entertainment industry, are particularly common in the highly specialized and "small world" of physical and dance-theatre.

Finally, boundaries are arguably one of the foundational tools of consent-forward work. The way in which they can be utilized in devised work is through a combination of methods standard in intimacy work as well as some variations that are specific to generative processes.

3.   Tools for uplifting boundaries in devised processes:

    a.   Presenting multiple options as often as possible to help facilitate a culture of personal agency

    b.   Model, expect, and celebrate "NO" "NO, BUT . . ." and "YES, IF . . ."[15]

    c.   Ask rather than assume

    d.   Boundary check-ins as a regular part of the process (helps uplift consent as revocable)

    e.   Sincere and active apology if a boundary is crossed

At times, creators are working on material that is very close to their own experience. Some specific boundary tools that can serve these processes include:

i.   Conscientious word choice, potentially incorporating options such as "work" and "colleague"

ii.   A separate journal for the project (separate from personal notebook or journal)

iii.   Noticing the specific physical shifts for a character and creating a physical practice of moving into and out of character body at the top and end of day

iv.   Scheduling field trips or research (including films and books) as part of one's individual workday, creating a more robust separation between work and recreation.

v.   Consistent, restorative closure practices

These offerings are "tools, not rules." Use them when you find that one or more will serve your creative process and your own integrity-based work. Some projects will be better served by some tools than others. Ultimately, as physical theatre work continues to be in conversation with consent-forward practices, we will collectively devise new healthful ways to create. I look forward to doing so with inspiring artists and educators as we continue to build a creative and human-focused field together.

Notes

1 Sarah Marshall, host., "Going Postal."

2 "Mission and History – Curio Theatre Company."

3 Stuart Jeffries, "'Actors Are Cattle': When Hitchcock Met Truffaut."

4 "Contributor Adrienne Mackey: Founding Artistic Director of Swim Pony Performing Arts." *Huffington Post.*

5 Margaret Judson, "How Do You Play a Porn Star in the #MeToo Era? With Help from an 'Intimacy Director'."

6 Tonia Sina, *Intimacy Encounters; Staging Intimacy and Sensuality,* 2006.

7 "Claire Warden: On Stage and on Screen Intimacy Director." *Actor C.E.O.*

8 "Trauma-Sensitive Yoga." *Transformation Yoga Project.*

9 "Trauma-Informed Practice Training." *Stockton Rush Bartol Foundation.*

10 "Tribe of Fools." *Theatre Philadelphia.*

11 Colleen Hughes, "Cultivating a Culture of Consent in Devised Processes."

12 J. R. P. French Jr. and B. H. Raven, "The Bases of Social Power."

13 Colleen Hughes, "Consent & Communication: Practices for a Stronger Community Theatre Culture."

14 "Foundations of Intimacy: Level 1, Class 3." *Intimacy Directors and Coordinators.*

15 Marie C. Percy and Jessica Steinrock, "Yes, No & Beyond: Consent in Performance, Lesson 5."

9

STAGING VIOLENCE & THEATRICAL INTIMACY

Sheryl Williams

I moved from Phoenix to Chicago with the idea of wanting to learn how to choreograph fights for theaters. I took every stage combat class that was available to me, and it was during my time as a stage combat minor in college that I was introduced to my first theatrical intimacy course – and I was hooked. I have had my own experiences of "choreographed" moments that were created in which a conversation about boundaries could have prevented a lot of harm, which is why the concept of theatrical intimacy as a whole blew my mind. My experiences were handled through a stage combat lens, and as I moved through my journey from in front of the table to behind it, for both stage and film, I have found that actors give more when they feel they have some form of an input and feel safe doing so. Since then, I have trained with multiple intimacy organizations, earned the designation of an Advanced Actor Combatant within the Society of American Fight Directors (SAFD), and gained professional experience in the field.

DOI: 10.4324/9781003319399-9

While continuing my personal training and following what information was available in 2019, I had an opportunity to use what I had learned from my first few intimacy workshops and my stage combat training as the Fight and Intimacy Choreographer for a student production of *Dog* by Francesca Pazniokas at Columbia College Chicago. I was asked for specifically because most of the moments in the show required stage combat staging training, but the synopsis from New Playwrights Exchange states:

> When Alice needs a place to crash after dropping out of college, her sister Penny welcomes her with open arms. There's just one catch: Penny's dog, Elmo – who may not be a dog at all. "Dog" is an experimental play about cycles of abuse, and the passive violence that keeps abusers in power.

And while I was doing my script analysis, this synopsis had me considering what stage combat meant and how my new training in consent and boundaries expanded what violence meant to me. I obviously had a lot of questions.

Trauma & Violence

Stage combat defined by the Society of American Fight Directors is a broad term that covers acts of conflict, danger, and/or violence performed for entertainment. A slap to the face, a fall down some stairs, an epic fifteen-person battle with swords and axes – all of these are stage combat. More than just set moves, true stage combat uses violence to tell a story, just as dance choreography, set design, or costuming can. I kept getting hooked on the word "violence" and thought there was something more specific I could personally expand on beyond the ideas of physicality. I wanted something more specific that I could really vibe with that included my new lessons in consent and boundaries and power dynamics.

To fill in some context for myself for the show, I began researching cycles of abuse, and it was during that time that I ultimately began to arrive at my personal definition specific to the idea of staged violence. Mixing the overarching concept from the SAFD, my own stage combat philosophies, and the World Health Organization's (WHO) definition of "Violence" from their World Report on Health and Violence;[1] this became the viewpoint in which I filter my designs. As stated in Chapter 3, WHO defines violence as the intentional use of physical force or power, threatened or actual, against oneself, another person, or against a group or community, that either results in or has a high likelihood of resulting in injury, death, psychological harm, maldevelopment, or deprivation.

Staged violence to me became choreography that is set to either the implied or scripted moments of storytelling where one or more characters display use of physical force or power against oneself, another character, a group of characters, or community, that either results in the illusion of injury, death, psychological harm, maldevelopment, or deprivation. Keeping in mind that these actions and results are meant to be an illusion, I found having that additional lens for myself added more awareness to the type of staged violence that is being created and how it may affect the people performing it.

In the *The Body Keeps Score: Brain, Mind, and Body in the Healing of Trauma*, Dr. Bessel van der Kolk M.D[2] says that trauma affects everyone and everything. It affects the imagination, and it is intolerable and unbearable. Everyone I have ever worked with so far have been very lovely people who I believe would not go out of their way to actively harm another being. However, it helps alleviate and prevent stress by addressing anyone's fear of hurting someone else early in the process. We may not need to know everything a person is going through in order to recognize that most people have experienced or have been exposed to some form of violence or traumatic event in their lives. In 2010, a report done by the Kaiser Family Foundation, KFF, found that

> Seven in ten (71%) 8- to 18-year-olds have a TV set in their bedroom, and access to pay TV and DVDs in the bedroom has expanded substantially over the past 10 years. About half (49%) now have cable or satellite TV in their room, up from 29% in 1999.[3]

And according to the FBI report for Active Shooter Incidents: A 20-Year review, between 2000–2019 there have been 333 Active Shooter Incidents across 43 states.[4] With the accessibility of information, the moment something happens, such as national, life-changing events and global phenomena, viewership is high. This plethora of information, I believe, has made people more aware of themselves and the system in which they live. However, it has also added a constant level of stress that cannot be ignored when designing and dealing with staging violence. We ultimately want to tell stories, not perpetuate the actual, "As-seen-on-TV" violence upon the performers.

Dog, Violence and Intimacy Work

When working on Dog, there were several things I had to keep in mind that weren't brought up but as the designer, I kept close to my chest. The character Elmo was being played by a White male and the characters of Alice and Penny were played by People of the Global Majority. "Penny" wore a protective hair style and was offering one of her own dresses to wear in the show. I believe it is important to be aware of the systemic dynamic that exists in the room between the actors who are interacting with one another, even if they are a cohesive cast. Additionally, creating a vocabulary built around consent that incorporates the performer's boundaries ensures that they feel supported and heard.

I also wanted to make sure there was a material boundary created with the performer's personal garment. Even though she had offered the piece, I wanted to make sure she was truly alright with accepting all responsibility if something happened on stage to it. I like to be mindful when resources are volunteered. The performer was not doing anything physically active in the dress, but because it was her personal property and it was her favorite color, I offered a second opinion. I also had plans to have jewelry removed from her person, so I wanted to check in with the material and durability of what was being offered. We are the experts of those moments.

This also created enough space for the male lead to address to me his concerns about the weight of the material and what effect that may have on him as he pursued his character work. Even though it was not the technique nor the choreography that concerned him, he was acknowledging the racial dynamic in the room and did not want to hurt anyone. I heard his concerns and helped create a foundation of removal that would help him "clock-in" and "clock-out" for every rehearsal both for himself and with his partners. We also did a boundary workshop with the cast, grounding everything in Planned Parenthood's definition of consent through FRIES.[5] This workshop proved critical when it came to a moment in the stage direction where Elmo is touching Penny in a way that was written as "are you really doing that in front of your kids?"

We created movements that were ultimately controlled by the actress overlaying her hands over his. I always offered my ideas first, making sure they were clear before ever moving forward and still checking in as it was being rehearsed, ready to be flexible if necessary. We gained consent to remove items from her physically when we blocked the scene. The scene called for the actress' hair jewelry to be referenced in disdain – so I also gained consent for that. I did not want to touch them but I wanted to add a look that would give a specific layer of maliciousness to Elmo. Simultaneously, I also was sensitive to the fact that Black hair has been a target of discrimination and oppression of an entire community and did not want to put the actress in a vulnerable position if she felt that the action would be too close to a real life experience. She said she was fine with the attention to it, and I assured her if it started to take her from the moment then we could remove the action.

Then there was a non-consensual advance from Elmo after a struggle with Alice while everyone is sleeping, wherein she manages to audibly distract him before he can overpower her. I again offered my ideas and did not move on until both performers were clear with what I was saying. I taught them how to engage in a pressure test, so they knew where their limit was to remain in the moment, as well as how to share weight so they could take a fall together and take care to not hurt one another during the struggle. We created clear lines of consent and communication as we moved through the scenes and created cues for each movement so everything could live in natural timing. For both scenes I would have them high-five in and out of the work. With the exception of the fall, I built the choreography around what I call "sticky cue" moves. These are the names of stage combat moves where once the cue is on the body, it isn't removed unless one character disengages. The consent and boundaries exercises were built around the check-in and closure system found in intimacy training foundations. Being able to acknowledge the male actor's concerns and simply having something to offer as a tool made him feel more grounded as we went through the choreography. He could decompartmentalize and invest.

There are so many stories that contain such a wide range of violence. Keeping in mind the outcome of that violence when choreographing can help ground the scenes in authentic choices forged and fueled by character work. I have had many experiences since *Dog* choreographing staged violence. From small physical disagreements to sword fights, designing over Zoom, on Indie sets, and for the stage, *Dog* was the show that changed the scope in which I viewed staged violence. It reinforced that my new training in consent, boundaries, and global awareness simultaneously enhances the creativity in my designs, allows the performers to feel safe and heard, ensures the director's vision remains intact, and even goes so far as to make sure that crew was feels supported. Had I not done this show when I did and with what I knew at the time, I wouldn't have the viewpoint and the creative signature I have today. We have gone beyond it being about the story; it is also about the people telling those stories.

Self-Care

I credit the intimacy training I have taken for this philosophy. But even though we are a lucky few who get to do what we love every day, it is still a job. It is a hard job. There are goals to be met and some days this job can ask the world of you. On those days, offering ways of upping the self-care when possible is important. Designing to minimize the physical and mental wear and tear on the performers helps create longevity to my designs as they feel supported in their personal acting process. Knowing self-care tips or having resources available to assist is important. Note that I said support and not fix. I may know general fight psychology but I am not a trauma therapist. I will never say I can fix how someone is feeling about something, but I can try to support them through it as best as I can. A good practice is to always try to have a few local resources on hand that you can provide should someone in your ensemble request support beyond your personal capabilities.

Tips and Activities

These are some things I always consider when designing, and exercises I consider to be helpful in the classroom and beyond.

1. *Tips When Staging Violence*

a. As a designer, I am not excused from learning at the moment because I do not know everything. Use it and build from it.

b. When offering scene work, allow people to bring things in, write things to perform. Also, I love New Playwrights Exchange.

c. Always work from a place of consent that is freely given, reversible, informed, enthusiastic, and specific – FRIES.

d. Offer and be willing to be flexible if a boundary is created.

e. As best you can, be aware of the dynamics in the room, where you fit in and affect those dynamics. This should also be considered when designing any staged violence.

f. Stage combat is "victim" led, so whoever is receiving harm usually has the most control of the safety, if communicated and cued properly.

g. If you don't know how to fall without catching yourself or bumping knees and elbows on the way down or don't know how to teach a proper sustainable fall, please don't do it. It'll keep your body happier in the long run and I would recommend stumbling instead, and take an unarmed stage combat class or see if you know any stage combat friends who may be willing to help. Agreements about compensation are between you and them.

h. Clothing Adjustments: working moments where a shirt can be untucked, a shoe pulled off, some form of distress can always help amplify the story of a small movement.

i. Creating check-ins and closure for material that may be the realm of everyday; sustainability over flash in my opinion.

j. I also recommend mental health first aid classes.

k. Create check-ins and closure for material that may be in the realm of an actor's everyday life, and sustainability in movement should take precedence over complicated stunts.

2. *Recommended Readings & Resources*

a. I highly recommend the *The Body Keeps the Score: Brain, Mind, and Body in the Healing of Trauma* by Bessel van der Kolk M.D.[6] Though I know there are not a lot of books similar to this book now with this material, I think it is a great introduction to how encompassing trauma can be and what violence can do.

b.   There are a lot of resources and classes on how to navigate boundaries and find language to communicate consent. I believe the IDC 5 Pillars are openly available; they are a good guide to use when trying to come from a place of consent and support for the first time.

c.   Always have mental health resources in your back pocket just like most of us have R.I.C.E. in our heads for physical injuries. (Just in case: Rest, Ice, Compress, and Elevate.)

3. Exercises to Create a Consent-Forward Space

a.   Pressure Test: scale from a 1–3, 1 being nothing to 3 how hard I am willing to apply pressure. Each takes turns, with consent to the specific area in which they are looking to grab. A will begin displaying those pressure options and B can let them know if any of those options are too hard for them to receive. If that happens, A will readjust accordingly and try again. When they find an agreement, they switch, and B will then take their turn. This can now be used to level the intensity of engagement between the actors.

b.   Practice the Fight Stance: when engaging in staging violence, as a performer, you want your feet to be shoulder width apart, one slightly in front of the other and your hip bones square or pointed to your partner. Actors need to be able to see the places in which they can work, and the position gives the illusion to the audience of being in survival mode.

c.   Contact Improv: my "Sticky cue" Moves: Continue to always ask for consent before engaging. The set of moves listed underneath: The grabs, hair grabs, corps a corps, are the "Sticky cue" moves.

   i.   Grabbing: first, with using hands in general, always tuck the thumb in with the rest of the hand so that it kind of forms soft flippers. This keeps fingers from getting jammed and people from being poked. When grabbing, place the hand on the agreed upon place and cuff fingers around the area. You may then slightly remove the thumb from the blade, but don't wrap it around your partner's wrist. Your partner must always be able to get out of your grip without trouble (see Figures 9.1, 9.2, and 9.3 for an illustration).

   ii. Hair pull: after cueing B in some agreed upon way that can be seen or heard (both is best), A, using a soft hand, will move an open flat hand towards B's head. B will use one or both hands to place

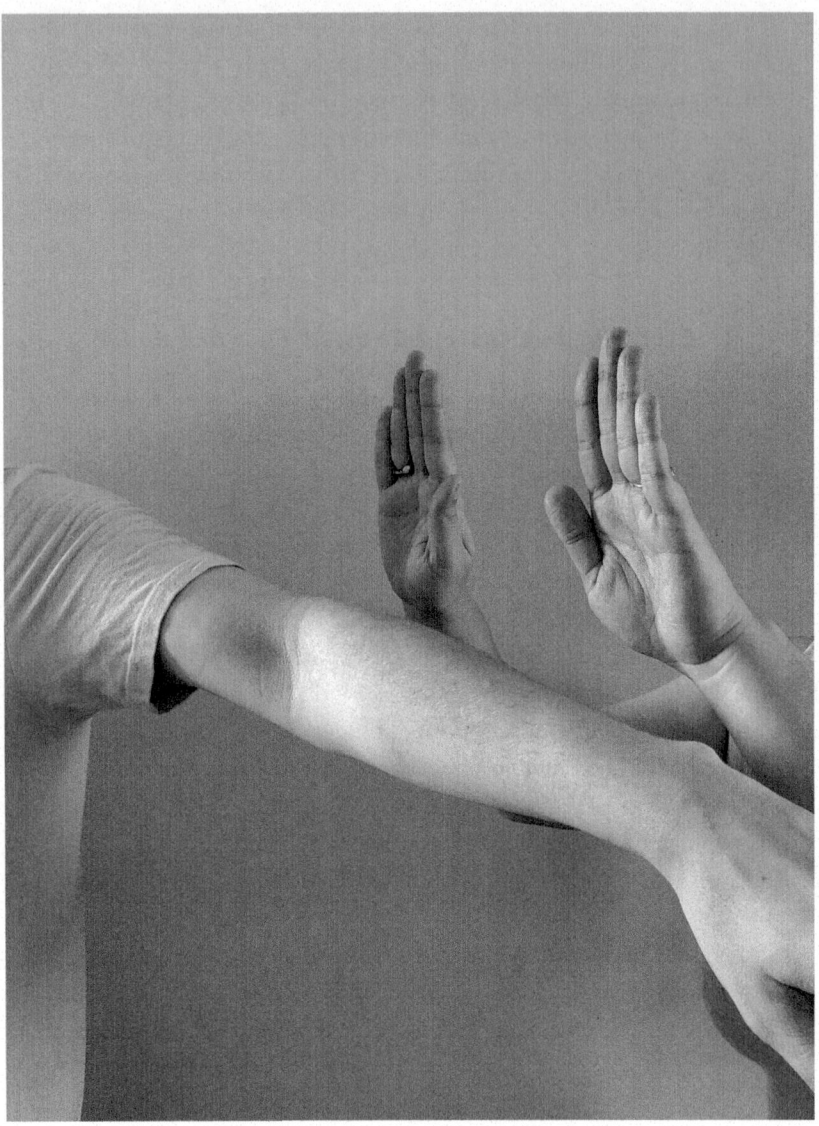

Figure 9.1 How to grab 1

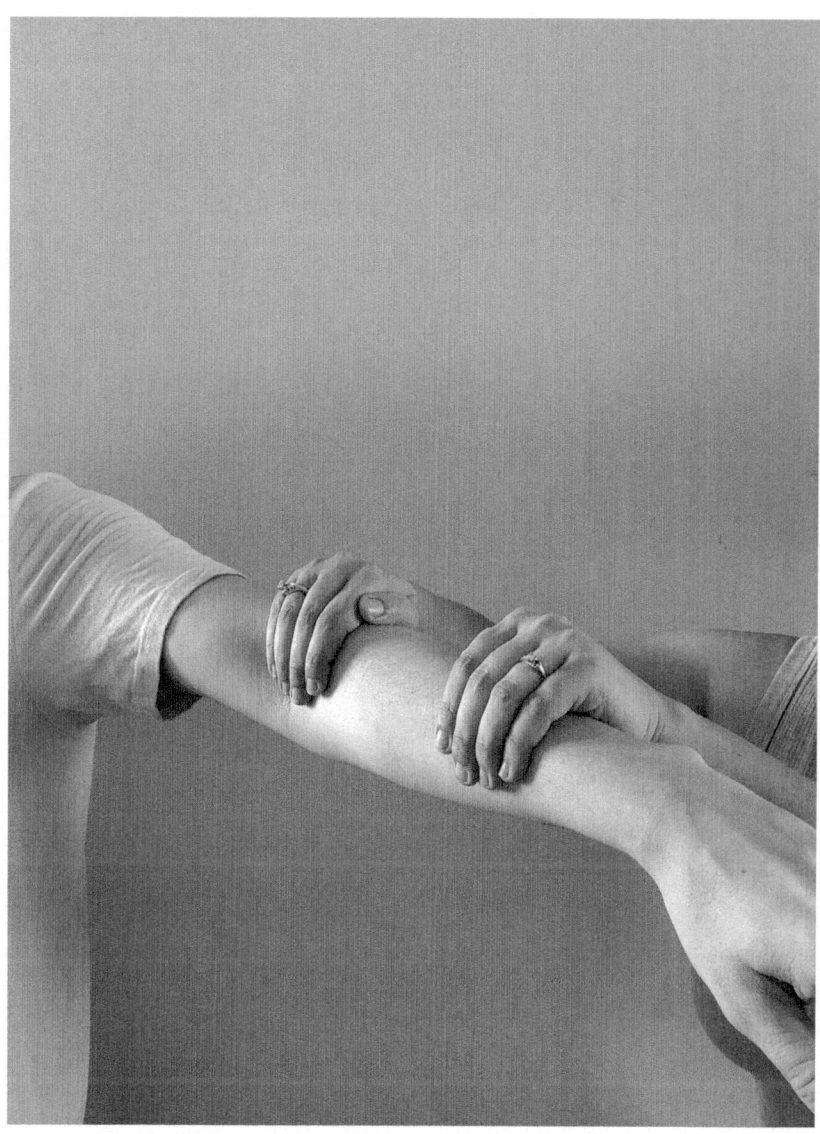

Figure 9.2 How to grab 2

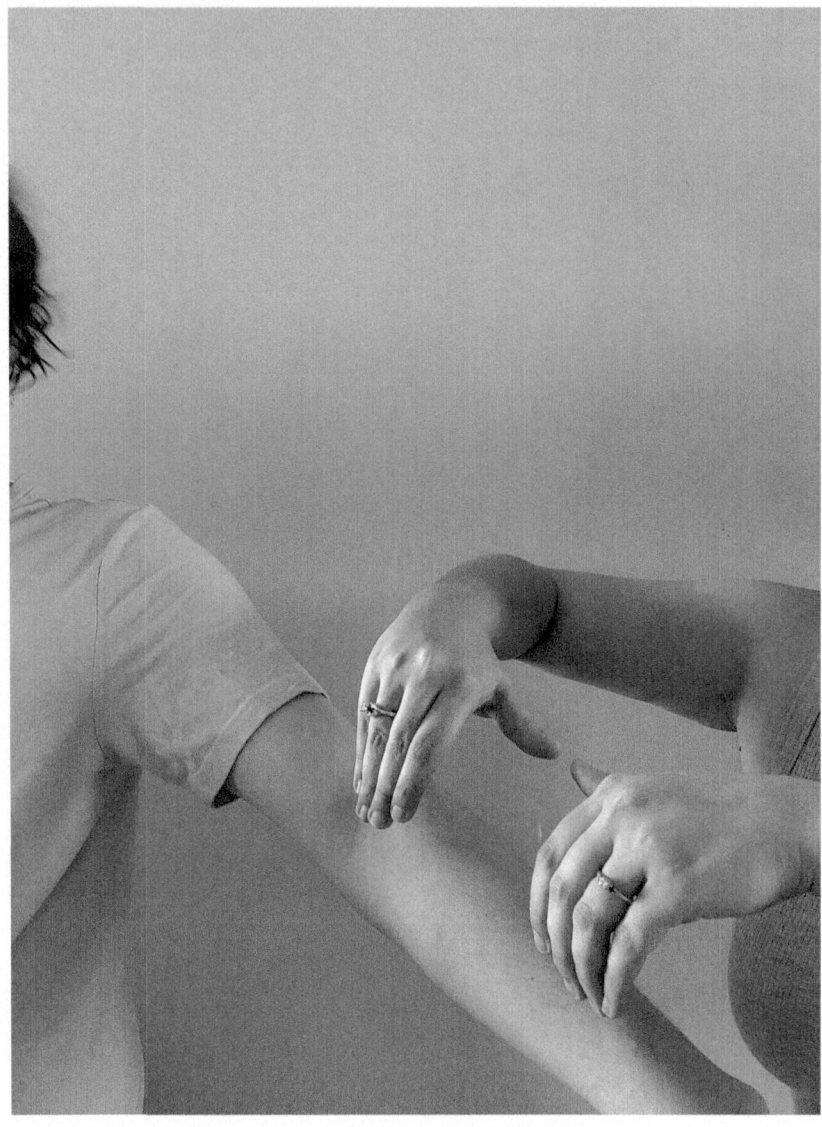

Figure 9.3 How to grab 3

Figure 9.4 Back hair pull 1

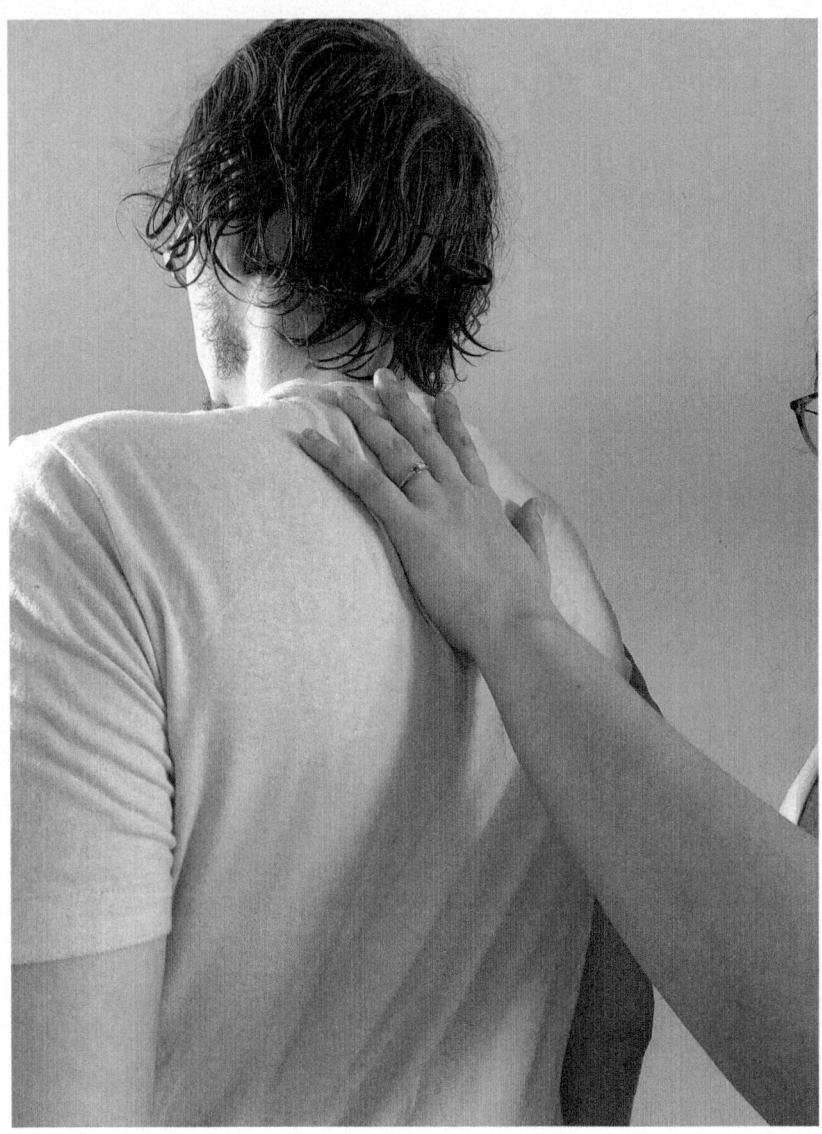

Figure 9.5 Back hair pull 2

Figure 9.6 Back hair pull 3

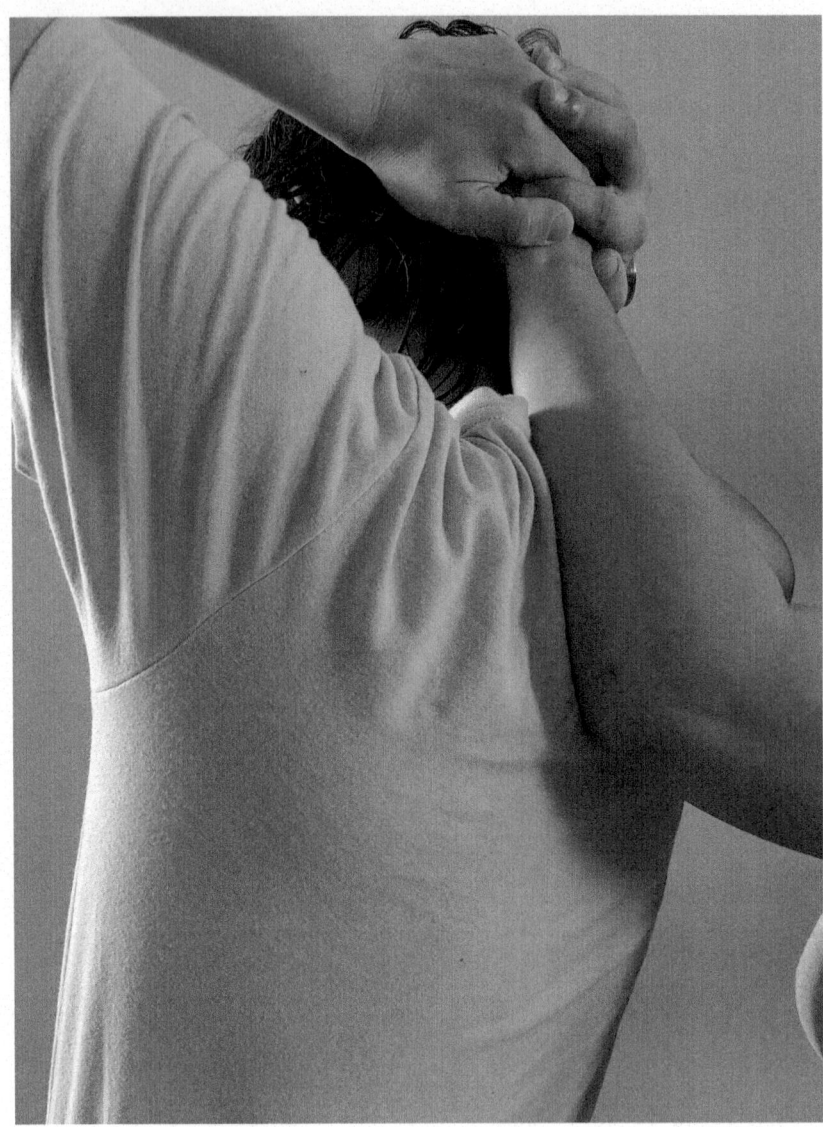

Figure 9.7 Back hair pull 4

A's hand on head. A will then form a soft claw on or within B's hair and B will control movement while holding A's hand in place (see Figures 9.4, 9.5, 9.6, and 9.7 for an illustration).

iii. Corps a Corps: (this is just French for: body to body. It describes the moment when the combatants come in close contact and the weapons are immobilized. It's a great way to get characters very tight for an emotionally intense moment.) A moves in towards B. A's left hand will end up placed on the front of their partner's right shoulder to protect A from their partner's shoulder bone – since this part of the body has less muscle tissue to absorb impact, we create a barrier with the hand. While out of distance, not close enough to touch, A reaches A's hands forward to cue where their hands will go, B places their right hand on As incoming left waist (agreed upon place around the waist). B's left hand goes to A's incoming right shoulder. B steps back on B's right foot and that creates an opening for A's left foot to step in. From there, they can push and pull the weight accordingly and around one another. This can move around the room; this can also be done with just hands interlocked with one another to maintain distance.

Notes

1 World Health Organization, *World Report on Health and Violence*, p. 5. https://apps.who.int/iris/bitstream/handle/10665/42495/9241545615_eng.pdf.

2 Bessel A. Van der Kolk, *The Body Keeps the Score: Brain, Mind, and Body in the Healing of Trauma*.

3 Kaiser Family Foundation, "Daily Media Use Among Children and Teens Up Dramatically From Five Years Ago." www.kff.org/racial-equity-and-health-policy/press-release/daily-media-use-among-children-and-teens-up-dramatically-from-five-years-ago/.

4 FBI. "Active Shooter Incidents 20-Year Review, 2000–2019." www.fbi.gov/file-repository/active-shooter-incidents-20-year-review-2000-2019-060121.pdf/view.

5 Teen Alert Program, or TAP808. www.tap808.org/consent.

6 Bessel A. Van der Kolk, *The Body Keeps the Score: Brain, Mind, and Body in the Healing of Trauma*.

10

ACTOR TRAINING AND CONSENT IN THE MOVEMENT CLASSROOM

Marie Percy

Introduction

Actor training is a vulnerable process. Unlike other art forms, the student actor's medium is themselves: body, heart, and mind. Pressure to make performances as "real" as possible can make it difficult for new actors to distinguish notes on a performance from criticisms of their personhood and identity. They are asked to take bold risks, always say yes,[1] and fail gloriously with body, heart, and mind all on the line. Many students emerge into the professional world having gained self-knowledge, confidence, and other valuable creative skills; however, many students will also experience harm due to boundary-crossing pedagogical practices.

Students are unable to say no and may feel that they risk being perceived as difficult, resistant, or not suited to be an actor if they speak up. Real harm is unwittingly done to student actors who are unable to clearly communicate their boundaries and protect themselves.

DOI: 10.4324/9781003319399-10

Got Your Back's 2018 National Survey highlights the very real dangers inherent in actor training.[2]

- Only 15% of students felt confident that they could turn down a role that was assigned to them if it involved something they were not comfortable with.
- Half of students of color felt limited in casting because of their perceived race.
- Nearly half of students experienced considerable mental health problems during their training with a fourfold increase in the worst mental health issues.
- 70% of students felt a teacher's methods were reckless towards student mental health.
- Less than half of students who were asked to perform fully or partially undressed felt able to say no.
- 81% of students were required to take part in exercises, scenes, or plays which required them to engage in kissing or other physical intimacy with a partner. Half of the respondents did not have the ability to opt out.

These statistics demonstrate that real harm is being done in acting training programs, and that student's dignity, identity, personhood, and mental health are all under attack.

I have witnessed and experienced similar trends in the ten years I have been training actors in American BFA and MFA programs. I began teaching movement for actors at 25, and as a young White Latina woman teaching among older White male academics, I identified more with my students' experiences than my colleagues'. Students dealt with tremendous pressure, overloaded schedules, and the fear of disappointing anyone, and they often dragged themselves into my class exhausted and unprepared.

Teaching is like trying to push a string across a table. It simply doesn't work if the student on the other side isn't pulling the string toward them. The more power, agency, acknowledgement of their humanity, and structured freedom I gave students, the more they prioritized their work in my class despite their busy schedule. I rediscovered what bell hooks had written about engaged pedagogy and its emphasis on well-being: "To teach in a manner that respects and cares for the souls of our students is essential if we are to provide the necessary conditions where learning can most deeply and intimately begin."[3] The greatest gift you can give students is agency over themselves.

As a woman movement expert with whom many students felt safe and heard,[4] I was often asked to choreograph intimacy for our departmental productions. I attended Intimacy Directors International's first pedagogy intensive in 2018 and found that my pedagogical and choreographic approach dovetailed perfectly with what I learned there. Engaged and transgressive pedagogy are complementary to the foundations of best practices for intimacy, and together they can be exponentially transformative.

What follows in this chapter comes directly from my professional experience and my ongoing collaborations with Intimacy Professionals. I argue structural change is *essential* for integrating consent and bodily autonomy into the acting classroom for people of all identities. I then analyze the necessary components for consent to exist, identify barriers to its presence in academia, and discuss pedagogical and structural changes to promote a holistic cultural shift.

Consent as a Model for Structural Change

Many well-meaning professors approach safety and inclusivity in their classroom through a benign but privileged lens: "I allow students to bring their whole selves to class. I listen, and I'm empathetic." This is a particular pitfall for established White, cisgendered, and heteronormative male academics. It is a privilege to be able to empathize with students' struggles without also making systemic changes to foster a more inclusive, consent-forward learning environment. Mere empathy is not enough.

During a Racial Equity Institute workshop I attended, the facilitator urged us to stop trying to pull people suffering from oppression out of the metaphorical river. Instead we need to go upriver and figure out how they are being pushed into the river in the first place, and stop pushing them into the river! Creating a culture of consent for acting students of all identities must be approached in the same way. Identify the practices, systems, and cultural norms that that push our students in the river, and find better ways to teach.

The acronym FRIES defines sexual consent[5] in real life. However, there are some important differences between true sexual consent and consenting to touch in an academic setting in class. I use CRISP[6] for this reason: Confident, Reversible, Informed, Specific, and Participatory. Confident replaces Enthusiastic because an actor can be confident and determined about their choice to perform a difficult scene without being enthusiastic about it. Participatory replaces Freely Given because consent cannot be freely given in the presence of power dynamics. In the following sections I will share the structural challenges posed by each of these characteristics of consent, and structural changes that can be made to foster that criteria for consent.

Freely Given/Participatory Pedagogy

Freely given is difficult. Consent cannot be freely given if it is coerced through real or perceived threats. Therefore a careful consideration of power dynamics is important to understanding this component of consent. Kimberlé Crenshaw's intersectional framework, Minnesota Collaborative Anti-Racism Initiative's definition of Systemic power, and John French and Bertram Raven's social bases of power can be used to create a comprehensive vocabulary for analyzing power dynamics (Table 10.1).[7]

There is no professor-student relationship that isn't affected by some combination of these power dynamics. This often leaves well-meaning faculty bewailing their inability to get students to share their true boundaries with them. Fortunately, structures that allow for participatory and collaborative decision making between student and teacher can build trust, open doors of communication, and lead to student engagement. Traditionally, decisions about grades, scene studies, learning objectives, and assignments have been unilateral decisions determined by the faculty member and handed down to the student. Allowing students to participate in these decisions necessitates giving up power over students, and instead engaging in power with students.[11] Here are

Table 10.1 Power Dynamics

Theory of Power	Definition	Relevant Considerations
Intersectional Framework	"A lens, a prism, for seeing the way in which various forms of inequality often operate together and exacerbate each other."[8]	A student actor who identifies with one or more historically oppressed identities will have additional real and perceived barriers toward Freely Given consent.
Systemic Power	"The legitimate/ legal ability to access and control those institutions sanctioned by the state."[9]	Institutions in the United States are built largely to favor White, straight, heteronormative men. Student actors who do not fall into that category will have real and perceived barriers toward Freely Given consent.
Social Bases of Power[10]	Legitimate - Formal authority within an organization Expert - Power derived from expertise in a topic Reward - Formal power to give rewards in an organization Coercive - Uses social, emotional, political, or economic power to gain compliance Referent - Power in the form of influence, popularity, or "guru" like teaching Information - Power created by controlling information needed by others	Most acting and movement faculty have all of these individual types of power over their students. The position of professor is inherently one where the power dynamic is skewed toward the professor. Without mindful and strategic structural considerations, these types of power can easily cause fawning behavior on the part of students, unclear communication, and unwitting harm.

practices I have implemented in my classroom that have led to successful student participation in decision making and contributed to a culture of consent.

- Develop the syllabus and learning objectives in collaboration with students. Draw three columns and ask the students to brainstorm what Movement and Acting skills they are "Confident" in, "In Process" with, or find "Challenging." Have a frank discussion about areas of teaching expertise, and how they overlap with the acting and movement skills in the "In Process" and "Challenging" categories. Offer suggestions on topics to cover that overlap with where the students want to grow. Collaboratively craft the learning objectives and topics for the course. Only work on intimate material if it's an important part of the learning objectives.
- Ask students to choose text to work on within certain parameters for length and style, or give students a selection of decolonized diverse texts to choose from.
- Use open ended assignments. Ask students to demonstrate growth in a chosen learning objective in a performance style of their choice. After viewing the performance, engage the class in critical dialogue about how the learning objective impacted the piece.
- Integrate mindfulness and Santosha when engaging students in critical reflection on their work. Santosha roughly translates to contentment, which means cultivating an inner peace and acceptance of the work that was done, while acknowledging that our attachment to the "perfect" outcome of the project is unrealistic and counterproductive.
- Use specification grading[12] or stop grading altogether. Got Your Back's 2018 National Survey has some bleak statistics about grading. "Nearly 1 in 4 said they didn't understand how they were being graded. . . . Almost 75% said 'yes' favoritism was a recognizable aspect of their training."[13] Grades have been established as counterproductive, diminishing student interest, and decreasing their quality of thinking.[14] Ungrading, as bell hooks calls it, suggests that we do away with grades since they are counterproductive to student learning. Some alternatives include asking students to grade

themselves, critical dialogue with them about their self-assessment, peer-assessment, process letters, and specification grading.[15]

Reversible: Providing More Options

The most common challenge to reversible consent I have encountered in my classroom is when students have interpersonal problems with their scene partner on a long term project. The good news is that if students are truly participating in decision making, they are far less likely to need to reverse consent. However, having structures in place that allow students to reverse consent opens the door for students to try something, discover a boundary or limitation, and change their mind and further reinforces a culture of consent.

- Use exit strategies early and often. An exit strategy[16] is a predetermined way for students to stop or pause their participation in an exercise or scene should the need arise. In order to normalize exit strategies, practice them often and thank students for taking care of themselves when they use them.
- Teach students the Discomfort Scale and guide them to use it to assess their growth. The Discomfort Scale[17] is a tool that helps students understand the difference between unsafe and uncomfortable (see Figure 10.1 for an example of the Discomfort Scale continuum).

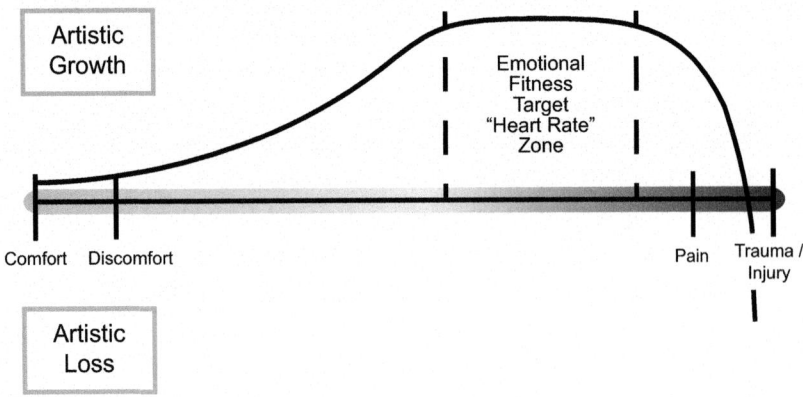

Figure 10.1 This is a Discomfort Scale, Image by Jessica Steinrock.

Discomfort is necessary for growth. However, if a student crosses the threshold from discomfort into trauma, growth stops, and the potential for psychological injury can cause artistic loss. The Discomfort Scale helps students assess when they may need to reverse consent, use an exit strategy, or challenge themselves.

- Use interchangeable scene work. Ask the entire class to learn both sides of the same scene. This makes it easy for students to use their exit strategy and take a break because another student knows the scene and can easily step in for them.

- Make attending class via Zoom or other video chat service easily accessible. Students need to be able to opt-out and reverse their implicit agreement to be present in class for their own health and safety. Put the link to your virtual meeting in your syllabus, and be prepared to use it every class. If a student is absent, set up the Zoom live feed, and allow students to observe and participate as best as they are able, no questions asked.

Informed: Constantly Communicate

For students to fully participate and consent to decisions being made that affect their personhood, they need to have as much specific information as possible. This is challenging because decisions faculty make without student participation are based on their years of professional acumen. Conversely, students have information about their body, their psyche, and their lived experiences which they should not have to share in order to get their boundaries respected. It takes both sets of information and collaborative decision making to chart a path toward growth. The more information faculty members can share with students before they participate in decision making, the better the student will be able to collaborate in that process.

- Don't be a guru. When a teacher with extensive expertise encourages students to look to them for all of the answers, they leverage expert and referent power to gain influence over their students. This compounds when that teacher is working from the dominant Euro-American western perspective with students of the global majority.

The role of the master acting teacher places the locus of control outside of the student. This forces students to do as they are told because of the illusion that they can only grow by doing what the guru says. This fundamentally undermines a student's ability to consent.

- Set clear expectations. When setting up any exercise or scene work, let students know ahead of time what they can expect to encounter inside of that experience. Set up a container,[19] "a collection of boundaries that allows actors to work impulsively within predetermined acceptable actions."[20] It can include what kind of touch, movement, potentially traumatic topics, or interpersonal interaction is permissible or may be encountered within the exercise.

- Use audition notices and opt-in for casting involving intimacy. Audition notices should include details about any intimacy that is required in the script, as well as the director's vision for what physical actions may be requested of the actors to tell that story. Students should indicate an affirmative wish to be considered for a role of this nature. Silence, the absence of no, does not indicate affirmative agreement and is why I recommend using an opt-in structure instead of an opt-out structure.

Enthusiastic/Confident: When Students are Truly All In

I want to work in an environment filled with joy and enthusiasm, not stress and overwhelm. The confident aspect of consent helps me rest easy knowing that my students are safe. Without the verbal and nonverbal signs of confidence in my students, I begin to worry. Are they just saying yes to make me happy, or because they think they have to? Confidence in a decision on the part of the student helps me trust that they are honestly sharing their Yes and their No with me clearly. I can then begin to give more targeted feedback, trusting that they will say no or use an exit strategy when they need to.

- If you're not sure how to interpret a student's nonverbal communication, ask.

- Give students time to process. There are times when it is necessary for faculty to take the lead and directly ask students if they consent to participate in a staged intimacy. In these moments, it is important that students have a minimum of 24 hours to think through their options with all the information. This time gives students the opportunity to consider possible outcomes and be confident in their decision.

Specific: Context is Key

The specific component of consent creates freedom. It can be uncomfortable, but necessary, to speak about intimate stories with specificity. When the context, multiple overlapping relationships, areas of touch, and content to be explored are all specific, students can more easily compartmentalize and dive deep into the specificity of the work.

- Teach and use nuanced movement vocabulary. It's important that students have a shared understanding of what is being specifically communicated in an ask.
- Have frank conversations about the story. Who, what, when, where, why, and how must all be answered about an intimate moment in the same way we would answer them during table work for a scene.
- Include closure. Actors experience "a significantly greater proportion of romantic/sexual feelings across their acting careers toward romantic acting partners, compared to other acting partners."[21] Closure practices allow students to step-out of the relationship between the characters and to resume their student peer relationship and the specific boundaries that are appropriate for both of those contexts. Effective closure practices include these four elements: connection, breath, gratitude, and sensory stimulation.[22] Together, these four components help ground the student actor in the reality of the moment and disconnect from the imaginary circumstances of the scene.

Conclusion

A movement classroom that has successfully integrated consent is one where students have the specific information they need to confidently

Figure 10.2 Students performing at Connecticut Repertory Theater in the World
        Premiere of "Good Children"

Photo by Gerry Goodstein.

participate in making decisions that materially impact their humanity and the ability to reverse that decision when necessary. These decisions include but are not limited to the stories they tell, the learning objectives they pursue, how they are evaluated, and the physical touch and actions they participate in.

In order to fully actualize this culture of consent, faculty must disconnect their ego from the student outcome and fully embrace finding power with their students rather than power over their students. There is a grave misunderstanding and mistrust that I often hear from faculty. They are afraid that students will not challenge themselves or tackle difficult material if not pushed to grow. I have found the opposite to be true. The more I set up structured freedom, the more they fly.

See Figure 10.2 for students performing at the Connecticut Repertory Theater, illustrating an intimate moment choreographed by Marie Percy with two of her students, one of whom stated how Marie created "a safe and creative environment."

Student on the left wrote about the experience: "I was incredibly nervous for my role in Good Children at Connecticut Repertory Theater. As Ella, I knew that I was going to have to tap into incredibly visceral emotions and when I read that there was going to be a sex scene I became overwhelmed. . . . Marie made me feel so incredibly safe and comfortable. She assured me that I was in charge of my body and that I have rights as a human even though I was doing a job as an actor. . . . She (Marie) lifted a huge weight off of my shoulders when she came in, I immediately felt taken care of and that feeling held true throughout the whole rehearsal. I went from being terrified of this scene to having a lot of fun with it within minutes. Intimacy choreographers are so important in creating a safe and creative environment."

Tips and Activities

1. The Consent Circle[23]

This game uses a modification of a well-known theater game, sometimes called "Spot", to give students an opportunity to interrogate their relationship with saying Yes and saying No in a low stakes setting.

a. The ensemble and the exercise leader stand in a circle together. One person begins the game; let's call them student A. Student A looks at someone (Student B) across the circle and says their name. Student A is asking for Student B's consent to cross the circle and take Student B's spot. Student B can say "Yes" or "No." If Student B says "Yes," then Student A starts to cross the circle to take their spot. While Student A crosses, student B must find someone else's spot in the circle that they can take by saying their name and receiving a Yes. When Student B vacates their spot, Student A fills that place in the circle. If Student B says "No," then Student A practices "Breathe and Pivot." Student A takes a full inhale and exhales, and then says someone else's name. Student A will continue to breathe and pivot until they get a "Yes" and can cross the circle. Whoever said "Yes" is now "it" and asks to cross the circle. The game ends when the exercise leader calls a hold.

   i. This game is an opportunity to practice saying "Yes" and "No" in a low stakes environment. Encourage students to be curious about how saying "Yes" and "No" makes them feel physically and emotionally. What thoughts, judgements, and beliefs come up around saying "Yes" and "No?"

   ii. Students should be aware of how they are crossing the circle and how that affects the energy in the ensemble. Find a way to cross the circle that uplifts and energizes the room. They can play with the speed they cross with, the path they travel, and whether or not they make eye contact.

   iii. Don't be afraid to get creative when crossing the circle to support the player who is currently "it."

   iv. "No" doesn't mean that the energy of the game stops. It just means we pivot, find another way, and keep the creativity flowing while we find the way forward.

   v. Students cannot move from their spot until they have gotten a "Yes" from someone else. If they get a "No," they should practice "breathe and Pivot," and the rest of the group will be supportive while they continue asking until they get a "Yes."

   vi. This game is best played in at least three rounds that allow everyone in the circle to get a chance to participate in each round. Depending on how big the ensemble is, this may take anywhere from 5 to 10 minutes per round. After each round, the exercise leader should facilitate a discussion that prompts the participants to reflect on their experience while playing the game. Encourage students to use "I statements" to avoid generalizing their experience. This game can lead to deep conversations. The opportunity to verbally process the experience of the game is just as important as playing the game itself, and can take a significant amount of time. Don't rush. Explore the game and the discussion questions as an ensemble.

b. **Discussion Questions:**

   i. *What did you notice while you were playing?*

   ii. *What happens to you physically when you say "Yes" or "No?" Does your breath change? Your posture? Your level of tension?*

   iii. *What did you notice when you said "No?" If you didn't say "No," what did you notice when someone else said "No?" At the end of the discussion, invite students who didn't say "No" to try it and see how it feels in the next round.*

   iv. *What do you notice when someone says "No" to you?*

   v. *Are you noticing the impulse to move before getting a "Yes?" What's driving that?*

2. Specification Grading Example Rubric

This specification grading rubric was used in my 2022 Spring Semester First Year Movement course.

	Project Completion 3 total	Participation and Professionalism 28 total	CTLs 14 total	Final Performance 1 total
A	3 "Work Done" on the first try **OR** 2 "Work Done" on the first try and 1 "Work Done" on the second try	25+ "Work Done"	10+	"Work Done"
B	1 "Work Done" on the first try, 2 "Work Done" on the second	22+ "Work Done"	7	"Work Done"

Project Completion 3 total	Participation and Professionalism 28 total	CTLs 14 total	Final Performance 1 total
C 3 "Work Done" on the second try	20+ "Work Done"	5	"Work Done"
D 2 "Work Done" on the second or third try, 1 miss	18+ "Work Done"	3	Miss
F 3 misses	Under 18 "Work Done"	0	Miss

Tokens: all students get three tokens at the start of the semester. Each token can be used for one of the following: (1) an extra try at another time to get "Work Done" on a project completion. (This may be scheduled in or out of normal class time.) (2) Turn one Miss into a "Work Done" under Participation and Professionalism (3) Count as one completed Critical Thinking Log.

Project Completion: we will have three main projects this semester: one monologue, one movement analysis, and one scene. Each one will be evaluated on the following criteria. A "Work Done" hits at least 4 of the 5 criteria: Clarity and Specificity, Use of breath, Variety and Contrast in movement, Use of actions, Use of movement outside your habits.

Participation and Professionalism: in order to receive a "Work Done" for participation and professionalism for each day of class, students must: Arrive on time. Have all materials necessary for that day's class. Be in the dress code. Participate in class activities within the given options. Be prepared to work on a project in class. For those attending via Zoom, participating means participating on screen in the day's yoga warm-up and the exercises to the best of your ability. Please DO NOT come to class if you are sick or suspect you may be getting sick. Using an exit strategy will not impact your participation and professionalism.

Critical Thinking Logs: student's may write one CTL per week. In order to receive a "Work Done" for a CTL, it must be completed by midnight of the Monday of the following week, and it must contain an Acting Lesson of the Week and an Application of that lesson.

Final Performance: the criteria for a "Work Done" in the final performance will be announced when the final project is announced.

Notes

1 Chelsea Pace, et al. *Staging Sex: Best Practices, Tools, and Techniques for Theatrical Intimacy*. New York and London: Routledge, 2020.

2 Neil Silcox, et al. "Understanding Acting School from the Students' Perspective: Executive Overview of the Results from the 2018 Got Your Back National Survey of Canadian Acting Training Graduates." *Understanding Acting School from the Students' Perspective: Executive Overview of the Results from the 2018 Got Your Back National Survey of Canadian Acting Training Graduates*, 1 Jan. 2019. www.academia. edu/41692621/Understanding_Acting_School_from_the_Students_ Perspective_EXECUTIVE_OVERVIEW_OF_THE_RESULTS_ FROM_THE_2018_GOT_YOUR_BACK_NATIONAL_SURVEY_OF_ CANADIAN_ACTING_TRAINING_GRADUATES.

3 Bell Hooks, *Teaching to Transgress*. Routledge, 2014.

4 "Student Reviews." *Marie C. Percy*, 22 May 2019. https://mariecpercy. com/about/evals-and-reviews/.

5 Planned Parenthood, "What Is Sexual Consent?: Facts about Rape & Sexual Assault." *Planned Parenthood*. www.plannedparenthood.org/ learn/relationships/sexual-consent.

6 "Intimacy Directors and Coordinators Level 1 Course."

7 Jessica Steinrock, *Intimacy Direction: A New Role in Contemporary Theater Making*. University of Illinois, pp. 25–27.

8 Katy Steinmetz, "She Coined the Term 'Intersectionality' Over 30 Years Ago. Here's What It Means to Her Today." *Time*, 20 Feb. 2020.

9 "Systemic Power and Race." MCARI.

10 Raven and French. "The Basis of Social Power."

11 Brene Brown, *Dare to Lead Glossary Key Language, Skills, Tools, and Practices*. https://brenebrown.com/resources/the-dare-to-lead-glossary-key-language-skills-tools-and-practices/.

12 Linda Burzotta Nilson and Claudia J. Stanny, *Specifications Grading: Restoring Rigor, Motivating Students, and Saving Faculty Time*. Stylus Publishing, 2015.

13 Neil Silcox, et al. "Understanding Acting School from the Students' Perspective: Executive Overview of the Results from the 2018 Got Your Back National Survey of Canadian Acting Training Graduates." *Understanding Acting School from the Students' Perspective: Executive Overview of the Results from the 2018 Got Your Back National Survey of Canadian Acting Training Graduates*, 1 Jan. 2019. www.academia.

edu/41692621/Understanding_Acting_School_from_the_Students_
Perspective_EXECUTIVE_OVERVIEW_OF_THE_RESULTS_
FROM_THE_2018_GOT_YOUR_BACK_NATIONAL_SURVEY_OF_
CANADIAN_ACTING_TRAINING_GRADUATES.

14 Alfie Kohn, "The Case Against Grades." *Alfiekohn.org.* www.alfiekohn.
org/article/case-grades/.

15 Jesse Stommel, "How to Ungrade." *Jessestommel.com.* www.jessestom-
mel.com/how-to-ungrade/.

16 Jessica Steinrock, *Intimacy Direction: A New Role in Contemporary
Theater Making.* University of Illinois, p. 104.

17 Jessica Steinrock, *Intimacy Direction: A New Role in Contemporary
Theater Making.* University of Illinois, p. 167.

18 Jessica Steinrock, *Intimacy Direction: A New Role in Contemporary
Theater Making.* University of Illinois, p. 172.

19 Stephen Wangh, *An Acrobat of the Heart.* Vintage Books, 2000.

20 Marie Percy, "Key Terms and Definitions." *Consent Studio,* 2022.
https://community.consentstudio.com/posts/university-instructor-
theatre-key-terms-and-definitions.

21 Jennifer Saslove, et al. *Showmance: Is Performing Intimacy Associated
with Feelings of Intimacy.* University of Toronto Press.

22 Jessica Steinrock, *Intimacy Direction: A New Role in Contemporary
Theater Making.* University of Illinois.

23 Marie Percy, "The Consent Circle." *Consent Studio,* 2022. https://com-
munity.consentstudio.com/posts/university-instructor-theatre-the-con-
sent-circle-consent-in-performance-lesson-2.

11

VIRTUAL INTIMACY DIRECTING AND CONSENT

Dr. Ayshia Mackie-Stephenson

The COVID-19 pandemic impacted the way we do theatre, moving a lot of performance online. Yet, intimate stories still needed to be told. And now that we are recovering from the pandemic, a whole new genre of virtual theatre has emerged with intimate stories. In May 2020, still in the shock of the pandemic, I was contacted to be an intimacy director for a staged reading. Fresh Ink Theatre, a local Boston theatre company, planned on recording the show and broadcasting it through Zoom. I spoke to the producer over the phone and she explained the company's needs. "The director could use some help . . . there's a rape scene. Do you do virtual work? Can you help us?" I was excited and terrified all at the same time. How could I possibly protect actors online? What did they need protection from? Because of this pandemic and the need for theatre to survive and thrive online, I have discovered how essential it is for artists to build best practices of safety and consent for virtual intimacy directing. My story with Fresh Ink's production of *Maiden Voyage*, by

DOI: 10.4324/9781003319399-11

Cayenne Douglass, speaks to this need and illuminates the importance of building consent practices for virtual theatre.

Directors and producers who call on intimacy directors want to invite safer rehearsal spaces. And I aim to do choreography that is repeatable and safe in both physical and emotional ways. The virtual nature of theatre during a pandemic still offers dangers to doing intimacy scenes, especially without a professional. You never know what anyone's past was like or their relationship to trauma. The safety of actors is not just about the physicality of a scene – it's about their emotional safety too. Often, physical boundaries and triggers can be linked to emotional motivations.

Working on *Maiden Voyage* showed the psychological aspects of intimacy directing. The actors were in their own homes and still had very real concerns about dealing with intimacy. Normally, I invite the entire cast and crew to my consent workshop. However, this instance was a bit rushed, as the company was already in full rehearsal swing. It is always best to pull in an intimacy director from the first production meeting, so that the cast and crew are immediately versed in safety language. However, the company was not looking for a consent workshop, rather for me to come in and work with those particular pages where the sexual assault occurs. Before the rehearsal, I prepared as best I could despite the rushed circumstances. I spoke to the director, Liz Fenstermaker, and heard her thoughts and concerns. Liz was concerned about the topless scene and the dance scene, and was wondering how props could indicate shifts in focus. Most of her concern was about the "biggest moments" which were the scenes that led to the incident between the two characters. The director also wanted to know what stage directions might be read and "what actors' faces might be reacting to." She wanted to know what would feel safe and respectful to them and to the stage directions reader. I used her concerns to draft my initial thoughts on choreography.

When I entered the Zoom meeting, everything felt surreal; I was so used to entering a room with bodies and using the physicality of that to anchor my work. The first thing I did upon entering the Zoom was to introduce myself to the cast and crew. The director, playwright, cast (10) and crew (6) were present. Everyone introduced themselves and then we began. I started taking notes. The video amplified everything. Every flinch of an eye was a moment. Sound also mattered so much more than in a physical space. Breath was everything. Even just the clearing of one's throat became a thing. Seemingly small or inconsequential aspects of the "stage" became bigger. I was reminded of my film training, and I knew right away that the virtual nature of this play would make the intimacy stakes higher.

As usual, I communicated to the cast who I am and why I was there. I always begin with the pillar of Communication. I briefly discussed my training with IDI and that my role as an Intimacy Choreographer was to support their director's vision, the playwright's vision, and everyone's safety in the production, including the cast and crew. I explained that my goal was to create safe and authentic simulation of a sex act. I told them about IDI's Five Pillars for rehearsal and performance practice: Context, Choreography, Consent, Closure, and Communication. It felt really good to walk through this initial step with them; it was grounding.

So much of what I do in a live rehearsal room changed: the safety language that I would normally lead with had to change – the consent language had to change. The reason I couldn't use the typical safety and consent language is because that lexicon was built upon the premise that the bodies involved would be physically present. I felt like even though I was not doing a consent workshop, I still wanted to do a warm-up that implemented some virtual consent language for all involved. Following my outline, I decided to ask everyone to close their eyes, breathe, and send positive energy to the group. And I also gave language for when anyone needed to stop or take a break and had everyone repeat it at the same time. I then refocused the energy on the two actors in the intimacy scenes. I asked them to say each other's name and repeat: "your consent matters to me, stop at any time for any reason." I perceived this step as a virtual tap-in.

I needed to get information on how the actors were feeling about the show. I normally ask the actors how they are feeling about the scene(s) and any concerns they have around the intimacy. I normally take the actors aside individually and ask them these questions, so they feel like they can speak freely. Despite the open Zoom setting, I still decided to ask the cast and crew how they were feeling about the intimate scenes: "what are your fears and/or concerns?" There ended up being some silence, which as a professor I've been trained to wait through. Then each of the two White women in the intimate scenes shared their concerns directly and there was a lot of anxiety around what the sexual assault scene would look like. Since this was unknown territory, I decided to get even more information from the actors. In order to build Consent and Choreography from the Five Pillars, I asked: "what will feel safe and respectful to you?" I also focused on Context, another one of the five IDI pillars, asking an actor: "what does your character *do*?"

Through this project, it became clear that virtual intimacy directors are protecting the psychological safety of actors. The danger in virtual intimacy is that the criteria for reading and holding a room needs reevaluating. For example, body language can become harder to read. Actors can become very concerned about how they "look" and put on a performance before they are asked to perform. So continuously checking in with your actors and paying attention to facial expressions, sound, and lack thereof will be important to "reading" the room. Advocating for actors means listening to them.

I decided to begin with the center of the work first: the sexual assault scene, since the actors voiced the most concern about this scene. I refer to it from here on as the "rape scene" because the playwright and director were adamant about using the word "rape." From their perspective, the word "rape" gave an authority that the violation did happen and wasn't a figment of the victim's imagination; they explained this to the actors who seemed to be onboard with this language and context. When I asked if we could start at the rape scene, the two actors said yes and sighed with relief, and the director was also in agreement. And since what happens before helps to understand intention and informs the choreography of what happens next, I asked them to actually start reading from the scene just before the rape scene. I went on to suggest places where a prop could be used to represent a state of intimacy, to be more metaphorical during some of the moments of exposure. For example, in a couple of places, sunglasses were used to enact nudity for one of the characters. The director suggested the sunglasses in an email where she shared her concerns, and it worked well as an anchor for calling attention to the character, yet helping the actor to feel safe. Since listening is crucial to intimacy work, I used the director's feedback to build the choreography.

Preemptively, I made suggestions on what stage directions could be read versus what could be left out and why. The playwright was there to say what was important and in her opinion, needed to be in the reading. After everyone weighed in, the director, the playwright, and the cast, we moved forward with a consensus on exactly what would be read. One of the actors asked if everyone could turn off their video while the two of them read. I asked them if they were interested in actually turning off their video for the read through, while the rest of us kept our cameras on. The two actors and the narrator loved the idea. I thought this would allow for the audience to still be an audience while putting control of the intimacy in the hands of the actors.

As they read the script, I took notes in my choreography design routine. At first, the black screen was mesmerizing, and then sound took the stage. The blackout made the rape scene scary; it mirrored a disorientation and a lack of transparency in the characters' relationship. It mirrored the ill intentions of the aggressor. It showed how the abuse of power often happens behind closed doors with a person you trust, and how no one else gets to see that, but we should still believe that it happened and support the victim. The betrayal was in the victim's voice and lack of a voice, when she stopped taking full breaths. The stage directions that said "after the rape" gave an authority – a certain legitimacy and lack of gray area – to what had happened. Despite the fact that the actors were respected and protected in the precarious nature of this virtual scene, the filth embedded in non-consensual intimacy became even more clear through the concentration of sound alone. When the blackout ended and the video came back on, the spectator was forced to see things differently. So often with film, it's not about what can be seen, but what can't.

I asked the actors and then the director how the read through felt. Because the actors felt so good with it, and a major concern was how they would "look," I recommended that they keep the blackout during the rape scene and I helped to choreograph where that would begin and end in the script. We also dealt with a few other places in the script where they wanted some guidance. I made further recommendations about sound and what, if anything, could be on screen when the actors had their video off. I asked the actors how they were feeling and if they wanted to work through anything else. One of the actors stated, "I was so nervous about what this (rape) scene would look like." The other actor nodded, unmuted her mic, and said, "that scene was my main concern." The actors said that the session was "so helpful" and that they "feel so much better about it." "It" referred to the rape scene. When I was called in to work with them, it had not been choreographed, and therefore, the actors did not know what it was going to look like (or what they were going to look like in it).

I also checked in with the director and she thanked me. I went ahead and did a tap-out with everyone for closure, told them to have a great show and that I'd see them next time. Having received good feedback, I left the Zoom feeling happy that I was able to help them get through this difficult scene at this difficult time in history. I do think how an intimacy director can assess the outcomes of their work is an area that needs more research. With my experience in the field, outcomes are assessed by whether or not the director implements the intimacy director's choreography and movement suggestions. The more the director implements, the more the intimacy director can see how their work was helpful and impactful. Directors are typically not shy about what they do/do not like; this vocalization is important to the intimacy director's feedback and how they build the choreography. In this case, almost all of my choreography was used, minus a recommendation to omit certain language from the reading which the playwright wanted to keep because she felt it validated the victim and the sexual assault. I would not normally comment on text, but I was specifically asked to do so in this capacity. Seeing my choreography sustained into the final production was also helpful and provided feedback about the impact of my advocacy.

After engaging in this virtual intimacy work, I have recommendations for building safer and aesthetically pleasing scenes of intimacy. First, the consent language changes with virtual intimacy directing. If the consent language changes, then safety is affected and a dangerous working environment can thrive. One of the issues with consent language with virtual intimacy directing is that since there is no touching, so what are the actors consenting to? How can actors articulate their physical boundaries if physical interaction is not even possible? What is the "container" in a virtual space? From whom and what are intimacy directors protecting virtual actors? I had under 24 hours to plan for this intimacy work and had to develop an emergency protocol, but these are the questions that arise as I process my participation in this project. Furthermore, what is more emotionally safe for actors will evolve from project to project. What works for one story doesn't necessarily work for another. For example, I have another sexual assault scene coming up where I will not suggest a blackout. A blackout for the upcoming story isn't going to serve the emotional safety of the actors and also wouldn't work as well aesthetically. Context matters. It is essential for directors to develop protocol for virtual consent. In this virtual environment, language practices around safety and consent are paramount. There are many exercises that I do in intimacy directing that were not applicable with virtual work. At the same time, I think that giving everyone the language to take a break or stop at any point in the process helped the cast and crew to feel more empowered in the experience. At the very least, it told them that an authority figure cared about their consent to the work. Having actors verbally confirm that their partner's consent matters was also helpful. I would say go further and have each actor share their own boundaries with their partner and then have their partner repeat it. In setting boundaries, actors could reference their emotional container as opposed to setting boundaries about their bodies. I would say not to skip private time with actors. In the future, I would have a private Zoom room available for each of the actors if time permits. At the very least, I would want to have a private room to speak with all of the actors at once or just respectfully ask the director to step out of our Zoom (i.e. put him/her in the waiting room). Speaking to actors one-on-one helps the intimacy director to build a safer working environment.

Aesthetics in virtual intimacy directing speaks to the world of film, yet can be grounded in safety and the pillars of intimacy directing. In the cinematic world of online theatre, less is often more. Things that don't show up on stage will show up on the camera. The screen intensifies everything. Every flinch of an eye can be a moment. Props stand out. Costumes are more present. The acting is different. There is also much more to be explored with auditory potential. Sound is always important but can play a much more emphatic role when it occurs or is manipulated in a virtual space. The elements of cinema can affect virtual intimacy directing and impact the direction that an intimacy choreographer takes to tell the story with authenticity, the way the director and playwright intended. Although the tools have changed, the purpose of the work has not. The aesthetics are inevitably intertwined with safety and advocacy. And in a world with such unknowns, it is best to ground safety and aesthetic concerns in best practices. Let the Five Pillars guide the work. Make Context, Choreography, Consent, Closure, and Communication intentional steps throughout the virtual intimacy directing process and repeat when in doubt. I recommend the use of The Five Pillars[1] as a means to anchor intimacy work in unknown environments. In the future, I will explore how the other four Pillars can be applied to virtual work. All we can do is create the art that meets the times.

Tips and Activities

The following are for virtual intimacy work:

1. *Questions to Explore*

a. How will the Five Pillars operate?

b. How does the story shape and/or inform consent? Context matters.

c. How can actors' feedback (thoughts/feelings/concerns) be used to build safety? In order to build consent and choreography, ask the actors: What is that you are giving consent to? What does your character *do*? What will feel safe and respectful to you?

d. How can the directors' concerns inform the work?

e. What are the literal vs. symbolic possibilities of the piece? For example, perhaps a prop can be used to act as metaphor and symbolize moments of intimacy or nudity.

f. How can the stage directions be adjusted to keep actors safe and still share the essence of the story? Consult with the playwright.

g. What choreography elements are possible given actor concerns and the use of technology (i.e. video off, audio off, subtitles, captions, sound effects, etc.)?

h. Who are the BIPOC on cast and what do they need (ask them)?

2. *Activities & Things To Do*

a.   Create Private Time: the intimacy director should speak with actors one-on-one or as a group. Create breakout rooms for one-on-one meetings OR have the director and crew step out (i.e. waiting room) and speak with the actors as a group. Ask the actors what feelings or concerns are coming up for them with the intimate scenes.

b.   Set trust and human acknowledgement:

    i.   Use the "Ubuntu Healing Circle" (see Chapter 4). To do this activity virtually, treat the arrangement of participants on the Zoom like a virtual circle of connectivity. One student calls to another: "Tanesha, I see you." Tanesha: "I am here." Tanesha calls another student on the Zoom call: "Sasha, I see you." Sasha: "I am here." Do this until everyone on the screen has gone, just like doing this activity in a physical circle.

c.   Give an "out" (an option for consent to be fluid): for example, allow an actor to signal with the thumbs up emoji and then shut their screen off if they need a break.

d.   Establish emotional basic areas for "the container" at the beginning of production or during individual rehearsals, either way, check in about these. For example: A: "What are your virtual basics?" B: "I don't want to be called 'he'" A: "I'm hearing that you do not want to be called 'he', I will not call you 'he'." OR B: "I don't want to hear the 'N' word." A: "I'm hearing that you don't want to hear the 'N' word. I will not use the 'N' word."

e.   Virtual Tap-In: always start here before doing any work on the script. The purpose is to connect and establish trust. Communication and consent are the pillars at work here; so is choreography depending on the movements you use to Tap-In.

    i.   Set up partners in the virtual room. A looks at B, B looks at A. Actors observe one another and on the Count of 1, raise your right index finger and inhale together. On the Count of 2, raise a second finger, exhale and clap your hands.

f.   Virtual Check-In: have actors confirm that their partner's consent matters. I would say go further and have each actor share their own boundaries with their partner and then have their partner repeat it.

This may or not be physical and should be informed by the questions in Section I. Check-ins can also be between actor and director, or the director might just listen in to two actors check-in and confirm what is possible. Examples of how a virtual Check-In might look:

ii.   A says to B, B says to A: "Your consent matters to me, stop at any time for any reason and turn off your video."

iii.   A: What are your boundaries today? B: "I want to read scene three in a breakout room before running it in front of everyone." (OR "I want to do scene two with audio only.") A: I'm hearing that you want to read scene three in a breakout room before running it in front of everyone. Director: "Yes, we can read scene three in a breakout room before running it in front of everyone." Or "Yes, but we need you to run scene five first, how do you feel about that?" B: "That sounds good to me, thank you."

g.   Virtual Tap-out: always end here before leaving rehearsal. The purpose is for partners to connect again, acknowledge trust, and leave the work in the room. Communication and consent are the pillars at work here; so is choreography depending on the movements you use to Tap-out.

h.   Set up partners in the virtual room or use breakouts to save time at the end. A looks at B, B looks at A. Actors observe one another and on the Count of 1 raise your right index finger and inhale together. On the Count of 2, raise a second finger, exhale and clap your hands.

Note

1 IDI, *The Pillars.* https://docs.wixstatic.com/ugd/924101_2e8c624bcf3941 66bc0443c1f35efe1d.pdf.

12

DO'S AND DON'TS OF INTIMACY AND CONSENT

Dr. Ayshia Mackie-Stephenson

Do

1. Support and "promote decolonized intimacy education and inclusive hiring practices in the entertainment industry."[1] This benefits everyone.
2. Always work from a place of consent that is freely given, reversible, informed, enthusiastic, and specific – FRIES or CRISP:[2] It stands for Confident, Reversible, Informed, Specific, and Participatory.
4. Know that boundaries change; be flexible and open to this human fact.
5. Get an intimacy director, don't try to handle entire plays with intimate scenes on your own without being highly trained, practiced, and/or certified.
6. At least consult with an ID if there is any uncertainty about needing one. Don't make your actors feel unsafe and take on a scene that you are not trained to handle.

DOI: 10.4324/9781003319399-12

7. Allow the ID to meet with the actors when the director is not present.

8. Make sure the ID acts as a liaison between the director/crew and cast, don't use another staff member as an intimacy director, etc.

9. Provide an exit strategy for any intimacy/consent work happening in the classroom and within rehearsals. Actors must know that they can withdraw their consent at any time. (An intimacy director can help set the foundation for this, but teachers doing intimacy work in the classroom should offer their students an exit strategy.)

10. Set rules for the room (these are rules that everyone agrees to follow regardless of individual actor's level of comfort, i.e. no exchange of fluids, call people by their preferred names and pronoun). If and when a rule is broken, take the opportunity to have a one on one conversation to learn more about why it was broken (this could help you to revise the rule or be more clear about a particular aspect of it), to reinforce why the rule is beneficial to the individual AND our community, and to be clear about consequences. Community guidelines are also useful, just know that guidelines and rules are not the same thing.

11. Give preference to Black IDs for work that is particularly centered around Black lives or racial trauma. Same for members of the LGBTQ+ community, non-binary people, and other members of the Global Majority. Furthermore, give Global Majority IDs the opportunity to also be experts and work in pieces that are not culturally specific to who they are.

Don't

1. Assume that certified intimacy directors are all created alike. Some of us have expertise in working with race, culture, gender, trauma, healing, dis/ability, and/or violence.

2. Intimacy direct your student's production. Hire a neutral party who does not have power of director.

3. Tell actors to "figure it out" or leave them unguided. This is violent. Know that saying just figure it out to actors and students is dangerous. They need guidance. Use this book to guide you in your classroom practice. If more specialized skills should become required

(i.e. heightened material, a production, traumatic racial dynamics), then hire a professional.

4. Expect your actors to advocate for themselves or know how to say "No." Ask open ended questions, such as "How do you feel about his hands on your chest?" (Hiring an outside ID helps the power dynamic with this, as IDs work to liaison between the director, actors and others).

5. Think this work is just about choreography. As Theatrical Intimacy Education states,[3] "This is about culture change, not just choreography." That is why this book is grounded in consent and racial and gender justice.

6. Assume you know everything even with a lot of training. This work takes confidence (not based in ego) and humbleness all at the same time. This work is not about knowing everything, as Sheryl Williams stated in Ch 9: "As a designer, I am not excused from learning at the moment because I do not know everything. Use it and build from it."

7. Shame yourself if you commit injury; acknowledge it and repair it by taking action that benefits those you've injured. Do the right thing now that you are aware of your mistakes. Guilt is selfish. Action can and does help others.

Notes

1 "Our Mission" by Intimacy Coordinators of Color www.intimacy coordinatorsofcolor.com/about-icoc.
2 Intimacy Directors and Coordinators, "Level 1".
3 Theatrical Intimacy Education's "Mission." www.theatricalintimacyed. com/mission.

13

BUILDING A FUTURE OF JUSTICE & CONSENT

Dr. Ayshia Mackie-Stephenson

Start every theatre project with: how can this work end White supremacy? Let me tell you a little story of why this intention is important. I was asked to intimacy direct for *Hurricane Diane* at The Huntington Theatre in 2021. When I first met with the director, Jenny Koons, I loved her immediately. The first question she had for me about the play was: how can we use our work here to end White supremacy? Just like that, out of nowhere – like the play was about slavery or something (totally not). I was like, WOAH and hell yessssss!!! I knew immediately that this was going to be a journey I wanted to be a part of.

On the surface, the story didn't seem to have anything to do with race. In the suburbs of the Garden State, the Greek God Dionysus returns from the heavens in the guise of a butch gardener named Diane, who's hell bent on reversing climate change and restoring earthly order by seducing a band of mortal followers. So, yeah, suburbs and climate change and oh, sex – godly sex. Yet, in line with our objective to end White supremacy,

DOI: 10.4324/9781003319399-13

Koons also asked me to do a racial justice workshop at the beginning of my work with the actors – the afternoon of the first rehearsal. I did it on power and privilege. From the feedback I received, this helped the cast to treat each other kindly and to work with each other in ways that made them intentional about reducing harm. In the cast, there were a few actors who identified as BIPOC and they welcomed this racial-justice approach. This play may not have been about race, but the people in it were going back to their neighborhoods, schools, and elsewhere in the Boston area to spend time with their children, to interact with BIPOC people, to work as directors in community theatre. The workshop helped to create a language of justice in the room and beyond, and that matters. Koon did not have to do this; use your power for good.

In the play, only one of the suburban women was cast as Black. When her story reaches its climax, she too will succumb to the whims of Dionysus and she can't wait. It's clear from the character's dialogue up until this point that she wants Dionysus and she wants them to want her (see Figure 13.1 for how this Black character (left) revels in the joy of knowing that she will finally have Dionysus (right)).

Dionysus definitely wants her – yet, they must be invited. The Black actress' line to get the Greek god to take her is "Tear me apart." As I was choreographing this scene, I shared with Koons that this did not have to be a moment of "angry Black woman" even though a Black woman was cast in this role. Koons agreed wholeheartedly. I explored a range of emotions with the actor. I landed on asking the actor to further explore the joy in those words and in this moment, where her character is finally going to get what she wants. We explored the flirtatious and teasing tones possible with the scene and it made more exciting, playful, and nuanced which worked with the comedy's themes.

So, yes, start every theatre project with how can this work end White supremacy. Consent cannot be understood without understanding power. Although Hurricane Diane was not explicitly about race, it's important to remember that White supremacy is the water, not the shark.[1] White supremacy is the power in the U.S. that impacts us all. If it can be seen and named, then it can be resisted and subverted in everything we do. We have to use every opportunity we have to use intimacy directing for its intended good. The two biggest barriers to this objective are

Figure 13.1 Kris Sidberry (left) and Rami Margron (right) in The Huntington's production of *Hurricane Diane*

Photo: T Charles Erickson.

White supremacy and sexism, and the former makes the latter grossly worse for BIPOC people around the world. Race and sexuality are always in conversation. Therefore, the tandem question is: how can we use this project to end sexism and sexist oppression?

Consent is a powerful tool to end sexism and sexist oppression. Consent is liberation; consent comes from justice and is inextricably linked to racial and gender revolution. Consent is freely given, Reversible, Informed, Enthusiastic, and Specific. Consent is an agreement to participate in any said activity. The person *receiving* the action must give consent. Consent is a way that we can acknowledge our joys, transform our trauma, listen to each other, and respect people's bodies. We can't control our past, but we can create art. We can create a world with consent where we are allowed to control what happens to our bodies in theatre.

Gone are the days when an actor is told to just go "work out" a kissing scene, leaving the theatre feeling violated that her partner just stuck his tongue down her throat. If that happens to you, then say something. If that happens to someone you know, say something, give them this book. Let's be visionary and end the violence. In this chapter, I speak to the future of building and sustaining intimacy directing and consent practices that nourish and bring justice to our classrooms and rehearsal rooms. Knowing that our silence will not protect us is the first step in being present with integrity and building spaces where we are all included and heard.

What does a future of consent mean? It means we have tools to navigate the revolution of intimacy direction that has surged the field of theatre and other modes of performance – and we *use* them. Know when to hire a professional, why consent matters, and the importance of consent workshops. The institution of academia has such an impact on the field of live performance and film. For many young artists, academia shapes their foundational experience. Let's stop blaming the institution and recognize and act upon our roles and powers within it. Teachers are artists and artists are also teachers; let's work together and lead together and build together.

Actors are human beings and consent is not a chore, it's a process to acknowledge and understand our humanity. This book is for teachers,

teachers who are artists, and artists who are teachers, because at some point or another, most artists are put in the position to lead. We will not learn to cultivate a space that is safe and intersectional overnight, but respecting students' race, gender, sexual orientation, and other integral modes of identity is a great start. Once we can collectively see actors as human beings, asking for consent, seeking consent, will become second nature. Cultivating a safe space is about changing our minds about the binaries of "yes" and "no." It's about realizing that "no" is not about the person receiving but all about the person saying it, what they need, what they want, what they desire for where they are right now in this human journey. Allow yourself to let go of the negative connotations around "no" and allow it to be a door that can lead us deeper into true intimacy – a place where we can show up as our authentic selves and be honest about our needs. Allowing yourself the grace to say "no" in your own life will help you to teach others this practice.

A future of consent means recognizing that actors are human beings and being intentional about that knowledge. Stop compartmentalizing justice. Recognize that all artists are human beings and that neither I nor you are superior to any other human being – even if we make better choices. This book puts forth intimacy work that is based in human rights and consent for everyone as an act of resistance against the fragmentation of justice.

The future of consent is grounded in racial justice. The future of consent is grounded in gender justice. That means giving Black and BIPOC people credit when you take workshops from them and then write journal articles or trainings based upon what we've taught you. That means not talking about power, race, and intersectionality in ways that don't honor the fact that Black feminism and critical theory has done that work for you, for all of us. That means recognizing your privilege, acknowledging that it has done damage to others, and actively working to end White supremacy in your classroom, artistic spaces, and beyond. That means loving yourself enough to know (and show up as if) you belong in the room and at the table. That means not questioning someone's Blackness and allowing Black to be and mean many things. That means loving our brothers and sisters who are lesbian, gay, bi, transgender, and more, fully, without trying to change them or make them think they can't be all they want to be, including Black and gay.

That means no, it will never be "enough" until women are running the world. It's our turn. That means that actors are not here to serve you but that art is here to serve them, us and our humanity and our ability to be good to each other. That means realizing that a Black woman led us to intimacy directing and that matters. The more women and men and all of us can break the silence around violence and harm, the more we can communicate what we do want and what we don't, the more we create spaces where we are free to love ourselves and receive love from others, is the closer we are to feeling and knowing that liberation is already here.

We are all in this together, as we are all out there doing the work in our classrooms and rehearsal rooms. Intimacy directing may be a new field but it has clear intentions. This book is to acknowledge the ambitious and necessary intersectionality of the field and honor the roots of that intersectionality in Black feminist theory and activism. The intention for intimacy direction to open doors for consent and end sexual violence against women, men, and non-binary people is its human rights legacy. May we all have the courage to make consent so important in our classrooms and rehearsal rooms that no one will have to break the silence and say Me Too.

Intimacy directors are advocates. Intimacy direction is advocacy. An intimacy director assumes the responsibility of holding the room and caring for the safety of the actors and everyone else in it. To do this work on any level carries the responsibility of advocating for others – as whole persons. This book is no way a replacement for an intimacy director. Nothing can replace a highly trained intimacy director in your classroom and rehearsal room. Without a highly trained intimacy director, the potential for harm is too great. Yet, basic intimacy training serves us all. I'm so happy you are reading this book – no matter where you are in your journey, know that you reading this can make a difference.

Change is possible with collective action. As teachers and artists, let us be reminded of and live by the sacred Yoruba text of West Africa, the Odu Ifa, "the fundamental meaning and mission of human life is to constantly bring good in the world and not let any good be lost."[2] If we do this, if we all start every theatre project with: how can this work bring good into the world? – how can this work end White supremacy? How can this work end sexism? – then imagine our classrooms, our country, our world in 10 years, 50 years, 100 years . . . the thought of this fills me with hope and joy. And I'm sending it your way. Let's make justice contagious.

Love and light, Dr. Ayshia

Notes

1 The Humanize Podcast, "White Supremacy is Not the Shark." www.youtube.com/watch?v=BDYWorrU7LI.
2 Dr. Maulana Karenga, Ibid.

BIBLIOGRAPHY AND RESOURCES

Additional Resources

- New Playwrights Exchange. https://newplayexchange.org
- *On Combat, The Psychology and Physiology of Deadly Conflict in War and in Peace,* a book by Lt. Col. Dave Grossman. According to Charlie Baker, "it is an insightful viewpoint, and I think it's a great way to expand the viewpoint of how conflict in scenes operate."
- More on the Five Pillars: www.theatreartlife.com/one-and-done/5-cs-intimacy-conversation-siobhan-richardson/
- For more information on working with transgender and non-binary people: Amanzi, Zel. "TTI: Trainings by Trans & Non-Binary Educators." *Transgender Training Institute, Inc.,* www.transgendertraininginstitute.com/
- Watch this documentary by leading trans creatives and thinkers: Feder, Sam, director. *Disclosure. Netflix,* 2020. www.netflix.com/watch/81284247?trackId=255824129&tctx=0%2C0%2CNAPA%40%40%7C158f7fcb-cb1f-447f-906f-f9ef7bf341bd-
- Check out National Geographic for more info on the human race and "races" as a social construction: No scientific basis for race www.nationalgeographic.com/magazine/2018/04/race-genetics-science-africa/
- What is antiracism? https://otis.libguides.com/tlc/anti_racist_classroom
- Definitions of racism and how it operates, tips for self-care, etc.: https://simmons.libguides.com/anti-oppression/anti-racism

- How to set a Confirming & Environment: www.youtube.com/watch?v=0BPbBPSVCFs&t=555s
- Learn more about what consent looks like from RAINN (Rape, Abuse & Incest National Network) www.rainn.org/articles/what-is-consent

Works Cited

Alexander, Kerri Lee. "Tarana Burke." *National Women's History Museum*, 2020. Accessed Sep. 2022. www.womenshistory.org/education-resources/biographies/tarana-burke

Apple, Michael W. "The Absent Presence of Race in Educational Reform." *Race, Ethnicity and Education*, vol. 2, no. 1, Mar. 1999, pp. 9–16.

Brewer, Nicole. "Anti-Racist Theatre: A Foundational Course." Nov. 2020. https://www.nicolembrewer.com.

Brewer, Nicole. "Anti-Racist Theater Workshop." 2021. https://www.nicolembrewer.com.

Brooks, Dwight, and Lisa Hébert. "Gender, Race, and Media Representation." *The SAGE Handbook of Gender and Communication*. Thousand Oaks, CA: SAGE Publications, 2006, pp. 297–318. https://doi.org/10.4135/9781412976053.n16.

Brown, Brene. *Dare to Lead Glossary Key Language, Skills, Tools, and Practices*. https://brenebrown.com/resources/the-dare-to-lead-glossary-key-language-skills-tools-and-practices/.

Carson, Anne. *Grief Lessons: Four Plays by Euripides*. NYRB Classics, 16 Sep. 2008.

Chödrön, Pema. *The Pocket Pema Chodron*. Boulder, CO: Shambhala Pocket Classics, pp. 66–67.

"Claire Warden: On Stage and on Screen Intimacy Director." *Actor C.E.O.*, episode 125. 6 Apr 2020. https://actorceo.com/125/.

"Contributor Adrienne Mackey: Founding Artistic Director of Swim Pony Performing Arts." *Huffington Post*. www.huffpost.com/author/adrienne-mackey.

"Declaration of Sexual Rights." *World Association for Sexual Health*. https://worldsexualhealth.net/wp-content/uploads/2013/08/Declaration-of-Sexual-Rights-2014-plain-text.pdf

Dyer, Richard. *White: Essays on Race and Culture*. Boca Raton, FL: Routledge, 2013.

Etienne G. Krug, Linda L. Dahlberg, James A. Mercy, Anthony B. Zwi and Rafael Lozano (Eds). "World Health Organization." *World Report on*

Health and Violence, 2002, p. 5. https://apps.who.int/iris/bitstream/handle/10665/42495/9241545615_eng.pdf

FBI. "Active Shooter Incidents 20-Year Review, 2000–2019." p. 6. www.fbi.gov/file-repository/active-shooter-incidents-20-year-review-2000-2019-060121.pdf/view

Florestal, Pascale. www.pascaleflorestal.com/

"Foundations of Intimacy: Level 1, Class 3." *Intimacy Directors and Coordinators*, 2022. www.idcprofessionals.com/pathwaytocertification.

Fredrick, Candice. "What It's Like to Be a Black Intimacy Coordinator in the Era of Consent and Political Resistance." *Elle*, 8 Sept. 2020. Accessed 2022. www.elle.com/culture/movies-tv/a33850492/black-intimacy-coordinators-interview/.

French, J. R. P., Jr. and Raven, B. "The Bases of Social Power." In D. Cartwright (Ed.), *Studies in Social Power*. Ann Harbor, MI: University of Michigan, 1959, pp. 150–167. www.researchgate.net/publication/215915730_The_bases_of_social_power

Gelpi, Madelyn. "Best Practices for Non-Binary Inclusion in the Workplace." *Out and Equal Workplace Advocates*, 2020. https://outandequal.org/wp-content/uploads/2018/11/OE-Non-Binary-Best-Practices.pdf.

"Gender and Health." *World Association for Sexual Health*. www.who.int/health-topics/gender#tab=tab_1

"Global Issues: Human Rights." *United Nations*, n.d. www.un.org/en/global-issues/human-rights

Henderson, C. E. "AKA: Sarah Baartman, The Hottentot Venus, and Black women's Identity." *Women's Studies*, vol. 43, no. 7, 2014, pp. 946–959.

Heung, Marina. "Representing Ourselves: Films and Videos by Asian American/Canadian Women." In *Feminism, Multiculturalism, and the Media: Global Diversities*. Thousand Oaks, CA: SAGE Publications, Inc., 1995, pp. 82–104.

Hooks, Bell. *Outlaw Culture: Resisting Representations*. Milton Park: Routledge, 2012.

Hooks, Bell. *Teaching to Transgress*. Milton Park: Routledge, 2014.

Hughes, Colleen. "Cultivating a Culture of Consent in Devised Processes." *Intimacy Directors and Coordinators Workshop*, 2 Dec. 2020. https://www.idcprofessionals.com/workshops#intimacytraining.

The Humanize Podcast. *White Supremacy is Not the Shark; It's the Water w/Poet Kyle 'Guante' Tran Myhre*, 2022. www.youtube.com/watch?v=BDYWorrU7LI.

Interview with Alan Goodman (edited transcript). *RACE – The Power of an Illusion. Background Readings*. Accessed 25 Sept. 2022. www.pbs.org/race/000_About/002_04-background-01-07.htm.

Intimacy Coordinators of Color. www.intimacycoordinatorsofcolor.com.

Intimacy Definition from Pace, Chelsea, et al. *Staging Sex: Best Practices, Tools, and Techniques for Theatrical Intimacy*. Boca Raton, FL: Routledge, 2020 with additional work by Kaja Dunn, Bliss Griffin, Ann James, and Laura Rikard.

"Intimacy Directors and Coordinators Level 1 Course." https://www.idcprofessionals.com/workshops#intimacytraining.

Intimacy Directors International. *The Pillars*, 2016. https://docs.wixstatic.com/ugd/924101_2e8c624bcf394166bc0443c1f35efe1d.pdf.

Jeffries, Stuart. "'Actors Are Cattle': When Hitchcock Met Truffaut." *The Guardian*, 12 May 2015. www.theguardian.com/film/2015/may/12/when-hitchcock-met-truffaut-hitchcock-truffaut-documentary-cannes.

Jones-Rogers, Stephanie E. and Allyson Johnson. *They Were Her Property: White Women as Slave Owners in the American South*. New Haven, CT: Yale University Press, 2019.

Judson, Margaret. "How Do You Play a Porn Star in the #MeToo Era? With Help from an 'Intimacy Director'." *The New York Times*, 24 Aug. 2018. www.nytimes.com/2018/08/24/business/intimacy-director-hbo-the-deuce.html.

Kaiser Family Foundation. "Daily Media Use Among Children and Teens Up Dramatically From Five Years Ago." 20 Jan. 2010. www.kff.org/racial-equity-and-health-policy/press-release/daily-media-use-among-children-and-teens-up-dramatically-from-five-years-ago/.

Karandashev, Victor. "A Cultural Perspective on Romantic Love." *Online Readings in Psychology and Culture*, vol. 5, no. 4, 2015. https://doi.org/10.9707/2307-0919.1135.

Karenga, Dr. Maulana. "The Mission and Meaning of Being African: Forging a Future of Shared Good." *Los Angeles Sentinel*, 30 Sep. 2010, p. A7. https://ibw21.org/commentary/the-mission-and-meaning-of-being-african/.

Kendi, Ibram X. "Book Talk with Ibram X. Kendi on 'How to Be an Antiracist'." www.aspeninstitute.org/events/gildenhorn-book-talk-with-ibram-x-kendi/.

Kohn, Alfie. "The Case Against Grades." *Alfiekohn.org*. www.alfiekohn.org/article/case-grades/.

Lorde, Audre. *Sister Outsider: Essays & Speeches by Audre Lorde*. New York: Crown Publishing Group, 2007.

Mackie-Stephenson, Dr. Ayshia. "Talk: Confessions of a Black Intimacy Director with Dr. Ayshia." *HowlroundTV*, Monday 15 Mar. 2021. https://howlround. com/happenings/confessions-black-intimacy-director-dr-ayshia.

Mackie-Stephenson, Dr. Ayshia. "Confessions of a Black Intimacy Director: Black Love and Human Rights." *Howlround*, 7 June 2021. https://howlround. com/confessions-black-intimacy-director-black-love-and-human-rights.

Madison, D. Soyini. *Critical Ethnography: Method, Ethics, and Performance.* Thousand Oaks, CA: Sage, 2005, p. 5.

Marshall, Sarah, host. "Going Postal." *You're Wrong About*, season 1, episode 2. 2 May 2018. www.buzzsprout.com/1112270/3884111-going-postal.

"Mission." *Theatrical Intimacy Education.* www.theatricalintimacyed.com/ mission.

"Mission and History – Curio Theatre Company." *Curio Theatre Company.* www.curiotheatre.org/mission-and-history.html.

Molette, Carlton W. and Barbara J. Molette. *Black Theatre: Premise and Presentation*, N Fort Myers, FL: Wyndham Hall Press, 1992.

Moraga, Cherríe and Gloria Anzaldúa, ed. *This Bridge Called My Back: Writings by Radical Women of Color.* Fourth edition. Albany: State University of New York Press, 2015.

Nilson, Linda Burzotta and Claudia J. Stanny. *Specifications Grading: Restoring Rigor, Motivating Students, and Saving Faculty Time.* Sterling, VA: Stylus Publishing, 2015.

Omi, Michael and Howard Winant. *Racial Formation in the United States.* Milton Park: Routledge, 2014.

"Our Mission." *Intimacy Coordinators of Color.* www.intimacycoordinator sofcolor.com/about-icoc.

Pace, Chelsea, et al. *Staging Sex: Best Practices, Tools, and Techniques for Theatrical Intimacy.* New York and London: Routledge, 2020.

Percy, Marie C. "The Consent Circle." *Consent Studio*, 2022. https:// community.consentstudio.com/posts/university-instructor-theatre-the-consent-circle-consent-in-performance-lesson-2

Percy, Marie C. "Key Terms and Definitions." *Consent Studio*, 2022. https://community.consentstudio.com/posts/university-instructor-theatre-key-terms-and-definitions.

Percy, Marie C. and Jessica Steinrock. "Yes, No & Beyond: Consent in Performance, Lesson 5." *Consent Studio: University Theatre Curricula, Intimacy Directors & Coordinators*, 2022. https://community.consentstudio. com/all-courses.

Peterson, Deb. "The Name Game Is an Ice Breaker for Classrooms." *ThoughtCo*, 11 Aug. 2019. www.thoughtco.com/ice-breaker-the-name-game-31381.

Planned Parenthood. *Sexual Consent*. www.plannedparenthood.org/learn/relationships/sexual-consent.

Price, Linsay. "Devising Exercises for the Drama Classroom." *Theatre Folk*, n.d. www.theatrefolk.com/blog/devising-exercises-for-the-drama-classroom/.

Rodgers, Janet B. and Frankie Armstrong. *Acting and Singing with Archetypes*. Brisbane: Limelight, 2010.

"Sara 'Saartjie' Baartman." *South African History Online*, n.d. www.sahistory.org.za/people/sara-saartjie-baartman.

Saslove, Jennifer, et al. *Showmance: Is Performing Intimacy Associated with Feelings of Intimacy*. Toronto: University of Toronto Press.

Silcox, Neil, et al. "Understanding Acting School from the Students' Perspective: Executive Overview of the Results from the 2018 Got Your Back National Survey of Canadian Acting Training Graduates." *Understanding Acting School from the Students' Perspective: Executive Overview of the Results from the 2018 Got Your Back National Survey of Canadian Acting Training Graduates*, 1 Jan. 2019. www.academia.edu/41692621/Understanding_Acting_School_from_the_Students_Perspective_EXECUTIVE_OVERVIEW_OF_THE_RESULTS_FROM_THE_2018_GOT_YOUR_BACK_NATIONAL_SURVEY_OF_CANADIAN_ACTING_TRAINING_GRADUATES.

Sina, Tonia. *Intimacy Encounters; Staging Intimacy and Sensuality*. MFA Thesis diss. (Virginia Commonwealth University, 2006). https://scholarscompass.vcu.edu/cgi/viewcontent.cgi?article=2070&context=etd.

Steinmetz, Katy. "She Coined the Term 'Intersectionality' Over 30 Years Ago. Here's What It Means to Her Today." *Time*, 20 Feb. 2020.

Steinrock, Jessica. *Intimacy Direction: A New Role in Contemporary Theater Making*. Champaign, IL: University of Illinois, pp. 25–27.

Stommel, Jesse. "How to Ungrade." *Jessestommel.com*. www.jessestommel.com/how-to-ungrade/.

"Student Reviews." *Marie C Percy*, 22 May 2019. https://mariecpercy.com/about/evals-and-reviews/.

"Systemic Power and Race." *MCARI*. https://www.ramseycounty.us/sites/default/files/Assistance%20and%20Support/Systemic%20Power%20Race.pdf.

"Tarana Burke Founder." *Me Too.* https://metoomvmt.org/get-to-know-us/tarana-burke-founder/.

Teen Alert Program, or TAP808. *What is Consent?* www.tap808.org/consent.

"There Is No Scientific Basis for Race." *National Geographic.* www.nationalgeographic.com/magazine/2018/04/race-genetics-science-africa/.

"Trauma-Informed Practice Training." *Stockton Rush Bartol Foundation,* 29 Sep–3 Nov 2018. https://bartol.org/tipta/tipta-teaching-artists/.

"Trauma-Sensitive Yoga." *Transformation Yoga Project,* 8–10 Feb 2018. https://transformationyogaproject.org/.

"Tribe of Fools." *Theatre Philadelphia.* www.theatrephiladelphia.org/whats-on-stage/theatre-companies/tribe-of-fools.

"Universal Declaration of Human Rights." *United Nations.* www.un.org/en/about-us/universal-declaration-of-human-rights.

Van der Kolk, Bessel A. *The Body Keeps the Score: Brain, Mind, and Body in the Healing of Trauma.* New York: Penguin Books, 2015.

Walle, Thomas Michael. "Making Places of Intimacy – Ethnicity, Friendship, and Masculinities in Oslo." *NORA,* vol. 15, no. 2–3, June 2007, pp. 144–157.

Wangh, Stephen. *An Acrobat of the Heart.* New York, NY: Vintage Books, 2000.

"What is a Theatre Director?" https://en.wikipedia.org/wiki/Theatre_director.

YSAFE (Youth Sexual Awareness For Europe). *Core Guiding Principles of Working with Sexual and Gender-based Violence,* n.d. https://ysafe.net/ippf/toolkit/part-01/chapter-2/core-guiding-principles-of-working-with-sexual-and-gender-based-violence/.

INDEX